Supernatural
RELATIONSHIPS

HOW TO GET CLOSER TO
THE PEOPLE YOU CARE FOR

ED GUNGOR

Harrison
House

Published by the Ministry Research Foundation
P.O. Box 278, Marshfield, WI 54449

Distributed by Harrison House, Tulsa, OK

ISBN 0-9624161-2-6

This book is dedicated to the love of my life,

Gail

As my wife and best friend of fourteen years (and the mother of our four children), her selfless support has been a never-ending source of strength. We still laugh, cry, and celebrate over our greatest project yet —— life!

My heart still thrills when I look at you, girl. I love you.

Edwin

"Many women do noble things,
but you surpass them all."
—*Proverbs 31:29*

How to Have a Personal Encounter with Jesus Christ

God wants every one of us to know Him personally and to become His child. The only way we can get to God is through His Son, Jesus Christ. Jesus said, "I am the way, the truth, and the life. No one comes to the Father but by Me." If you would like to have a personal salvation experience, ask Jesus Christ into your heart. Pray this simple prayer out loud to God and mean it from your heart:

> "Lord Jesus, I know that I'm a sinner. I realize that I can't make it on my own. Thank You for dying for me. Right at this moment, the best way I know how, I trust You as my Savior and Lord. According to the Bible (Romans 10:9-10), I am now saved. I can know You intimately now. In Jesus' name. Amen."

Now you are ready to experience God's power in order to secure *Supernatural Relationships* in your life!

*(If you have just received Jesus and would like more information on what to do next, please write to Ed Gungor today. He will send you his book entitled **Turning Point: Getting Started in Your New Life with Jesus**, at no charge. You can find Ed's address at the back of this book.)*

TABLE OF CONTENTS

INTRODUCTION

A man once said, "The more I get to know some people, the better I like my dog." That seems to capture how we feel after we experience conflict with each other.

The disillusioned wife says, "I don't know . . . it seems we started out so beautifully. We never argued or fought. I thought we had something special. Now we can't stand each other!"

The disgruntled employee says, "When I first started working here I was excited about it. The people I worked for really seemed to care — boy, was I blind! Now I really see what they are like!"

The church member says, "Love? There is no love in this church. Sure, I used to think it was there, but now I know people in the church. They are a bunch of hypocrites!"

These familiar stories lead me to the conclusion that it is easy to get relationships started, but often difficult, if not monumentally complex, to keep them going. Just as sure as the sun will rise tomorrow, conflict will appear in every relationship. Jesus said, "Offenses will come."

We all want to be close to and understood by the people with whom we work and live, but intimacy is costly. In fact, there is no such thing as intimacy without conflict. Intimacy is *forged* in the furnace of conflict. The reason so few of us experience intimacy with others is because we do not know how to deal with conflict when it comes — so we run.

Most failures in employer/employee relationships, marriages, family relationships, pastor/staff relationships, and churches could have been avoided. The problem is that we have little understanding of how to get along with each other. Long-term relationships are quickly becoming a thing of the past.

We blame the devil — and he certainly plays a vital, destructive role — but Satan isn't the only one with whom we must deal. We must learn the strategies that build our relationships with others instead of practicing the ones that destroy them. We must discover what **we must do** to win on this battlefield!

This book is about winning in our relationships. As you put the truths you read into practice, you will discover the power you have in Jesus Christ to build, correct, and restore relationships you were previously ready to abandon.

A Personal Reflection

Ten years ago, you would never have caught me reading a book on relationships, much less writing one. I enjoyed the benefits of marriage and having friends, but I wanted to have them without any real effort on my part. I figured relationships should just

10

"happen" . . . especially if they were God's will. Although I loved those close to me, I focused my attention on *doing something important* for God, not in maintaining or enriching the relationships I already had.

I was "on fire" for God. I wanted to reach "the world" for Christ, not those whom I already knew. I felt compelled to reach out to those I did not know in response to God's command to "go ye into all the world." I was certain that this was the most important verse in the Bible.

For me, Jesus' command to "forsake all" and follow Him translated into a life committed to touching those I could know on a *ministry* level, not a personal one. It seemed that Jesus encouraged this thinking when He said things like, "He who loves father or mother more than Me is not worthy of Me: and he who loves son or daughter more than Me is not worthy of Me."

It did not dawn on me for years that in this, and other similar verses, Jesus was talking about our initial salvation experience. He was saying if we refuse to accept Him as Savior because our parents, or spouses, or children, or whoever, would be offended, we are not worthy of Him.

He was not saying that we are to adopt a lifestyle that disregards those closest to us — those whom God had sovereignly placed into our lives. Actually, those closest to us are a big part of the world to which we are called to go!

It took a visitation from God to capture my interest in the subject of relationships. This book is a result of the events and illuminations God brought to me in the years that have followed. The truths presented here have been proven in my life and in the lives of those God has allowed me to influence.

A Key to Evangelization

Today I am convinced more than ever that learning *how* to build and restore relationships is one of the greatest tools available to the Body of Christ for touching our world and for fulfilling our individual destinies.

A California newspaper carried an ad promoting an agency that offered to send out a "friend" at a moments notice. This "friend" would be available to sit and chat with you if you were lonely, or hold your hand if you were dying. As long as you were willing to pay for the service, they were willing to continue the friendship.

It seems we are living in a nation that has lost the ability to develop meaningful relationships. Individuality, independence, and privacy have replaced concepts of community and sharing. Somehow we have become convinced that every man *is an island*!

Our "rat-race" society has alienated us from each other. Marriages are failing —— millions of children are living with only one biological parent —— people are lonely.

Sad to say, this "rat race" mentality has even affected the Church. Where is the Church in a world where elderly people are so lonely that they call "Information" and "Time" on their telephones, just to hear recorded human voices? Have we abdicated our responsibility to touch hurting humanity to those in the professional ministry? Have we thought those called to do "mass evangelism" through the media and rallies will do the whole job? Thank God for what they are doing, but we must *all* do our part if God is going to rescue the lost of our world.

If the Church in America will learn how to develop and maintain effective relationships with others, we can win America. One of the greatest needs of the individuals who live in America is for someone to love and appreciate them — to really care!

Recently, I read of a young University of Miami student who was found dead in his apartment off campus. He was last seen alive before the Thanksgiving break — they found his body in January! No one even missed him over Christmas! They found two eviction notices on his door and the TV was still on. He needed someone to care. We need to learn *how*. If the Church will rise to meet the needs of those within her scope of influence, there will be great revival in our land.

Get ready to be challenged. This book contains a lot of information about what *you* can do to make your relationships work. But let me warn you. Don't try to apply everything you learn at once. We need the Holy Spirit to "guide us into all truth" (John 16:13) or we will be overwhelmed by it. Remember that Christianity is a *supernatural* lifestyle. Keep this in mind as you read because God's commands for relationships may seem too difficult for you to follow. When you come to places like that, look beyond yourself and ask Him to help you.

"[Not in your own strength] for it is God Who is all the while effectually **at work in you** — energizing and creating in you the power and desire — both to will and to work for His good pleasure and satisfaction and delight." (Philippians 2:13 AMP)

It is **His work in us** that will enable us to experience *Supernatural Relationships*.

Ed Gungor
Marshfield, Wisconsin

14

I lift up my eyes to the hills
    where does my help come from?
My help comes from the Lord,
    the Maker of heaven and earth.
Ps 121:1 NIV

1

THE VISITATION

As a young pastor, I spent the bulk of my time studying, interceding in prayer, counseling, preaching, and praying for miracles. I lived, longing for the spectacular. I was so intense, you would have thought I was shooting to win the whole world to Christ *by the weekend.*

Though I loved my family with all my heart, I had a difficult time justifying "casual" time with them. "After all," I'd reason, "people were going to hell and I need to stay close to God. I can't get too tangled up with *natural* things."

My greatest dread was my "day off." That was a day I was to stay home and do "regular stuff." Although my wife Gail looked forward to these days, they were like a scourge to me. I would rather be praying, preparing, and getting strategies to effect the world-at-large than taking out the garbage, tumbling on the floor with our toddler, or going hunting at the mall with Gail. On those days, I would often exasperate her because she sensed that I was somewhere else mentally.

I realized God expected me to service my relationship with my family, and I really loved them. But it seemed to me that God valued ministry over garbage removal, play time, and casual chatter. There was never any question that if someone needed me to minister, pray, counsel or preach to them, I must lay my day off "at the altar" to follow God's call.

Then came the day in the spring of '82 that would forever change the way I saw things.

I woke up late that morning and didn't get my prayer and study time in before the family was up and about. I knew if I were to run off to study and pray, it would look to Gail like another work day. So I stayed home and started participating in what was happening around the house — though I was feeling a little disappointed and a little short on patience for not getting my devotional time.

I kept mentally beating myself thinking, "I should have gotten up earlier — how can I expect to win the world for Christ if I am not consistent in my devotional time?!"

Then I would catch myself, "Forget it for now, Edwin, you're supposed to focus on family stuff for now — you can pray later."

By noon I had helped clean up the house; had some conversation over coffee with Gail; fed, changed and started rocking Michael, our first born, to sleep for his mid-day nap. Gail also decided to take a nap so I was about to have some time to myself. Hurrah! That meant some time in the Word and prayer.

Actually, I was somewhat proud of myself. I had been a pretty good husband and father all morning and now I was ready to press in and be a good Christian *too!*

After Michael fell asleep, I laid him down and hastened toward the stairs, excited that I could finally work in my devotional time. As I passed by our bedroom in the hall, Gail called to me asking me to massage the back of her neck —— she had a headache.

I bristled inside! "Doesn't she appreciate all I've done today?!" I thought. "I've got to get into the Word! I'm a pastor . . . a spiritual leader . . . God's man!!" I knew she was my wife and had the right to ask for attention, but this wasn't the right time! I had fulfilled my natural duties all day long. It was time to "be about my Father's business."

Just as I was about to retort with "C'mon Gail, I've got other things I wanted to do . . . ," the Lord said to me, "If you'll do this, I will show you something."

My immediate response was shock. I usually had to wait before Him in prayer for some time before I would get the slightest impression, much less hear His voice. Here I was in the midst of frustration and feeling selfish about my life, and He was clearly speaking. On the inside I said to Him, "O.K.". I walked, somewhat bewildered, into our room and sat on the bed.

As I raised my hand to rub Gail's neck, something happened that I had not expected —— the very presence of God filled our bedroom. Thoughts raced in different directions through my mind, *"What's happening? Am I going to have a vision? Does she sense this? Why are you present like this, Lord?"*.

Then as I looked at Gail, she seemed more beautiful. This presence seemed to make me appreciate my wife more! I loved just sitting there being with her and rubbing her neck. It seemed important and valuable. I had been heading for study and prayer. Surely that was more important in God's eyes than spending more time with the girl I had married . . . or was it? What was going on?

In the past, I had sensed God's presence or *anointing* enabling me to articulate and preach better. I had been in counseling sessions where a wave of insight came to me equipping me to give godly counsel. While praying for sick folks I had sensed a strong *anointing* that enabled healing. I had witnessed to others about the Lord and experienced God's help to say things that I didn't plan to say or even realized I knew — that was the anointing. I have been anointed in prayer where I could feel a confidence strengthening and filling me with living faith and expectation. **But I had never experienced God's anointing to be a husband. I thought I was to do that alone!**

The Holy Spirit was anointing me to be sensitive to my wife's needs! But it was more than that.

I knew I was supposed to be sensitive to her needs before experiencing this anointing. At Bible school they taught me it was necessary to keep your home in order if you wanted to be useful to God in ministry. Keeping one's home relationships in line was a duty and an obligation — you know, like flossing your teeth and taking out the garbage. The unusual thing here, though, was that meeting her needs under this anointing made it leave the realm of duty and enter the arena of *adventure!* It left the realm of ordinary and not-so-important and entered the arena of EXTRAordinary and vital.

Romans 14:17 tells us that the kingdom of God is not just a

natural thing filled with *duties.* It is a place where ". . . righteousness, peace and joy in the Holy Spirit" exists. At that moment I was experiencing the kingdom of God in my marriage. I was experiencing the sheer thrill and joy of venturing out "under the influence" of God. I was tasting of Jesus' words, "I have come that they may have life, and **have it to the full**." John 10:10. This was *more than* fulfilling my responsibility as a husband. This was full, robust life!

Because of its importance, the ministry has always been a thrill. I always experience a deep sense of purpose and satisfaction when I sense God's presence touching others through me. It has never been a dull or boring thing to follow God. It has been an adventure!

Home life, on the other hand, seemed pretty mundane by comparison. It had always been part of the "daily grind" of responsibility. But my whole viewpoint changed that afternoon. For God to speak to me in such a dramatic way made me realize that it was a very important area to Him.

There is an enablement, or anointing, for us as spouses, parents, children, employees, employers, etc. We need His anointing in our everyday relationships as desperately as we need His anointing to reach out to the world-at-large.

The God who said, "Go ye into all the world and preach the Gospel to all creation" was the same God who said, "Husbands love your wives," "Fathers, do not provoke your children," "Be kind to one another," etc.

The Scriptures teach us that whatever God has called us to do, He will equip us to do (Hebrews 13:21). We eagerly seek and pray for His anointing to minister, heal, and set men free — but

19

most have not discovered His anointing to get along with others. Yet, the call to love those close to us is just as real and important as the call to reach those whom we don't know. I now know that the anointing to minister to those close to us is as real and necessary as the anointing to minister to those with whom we have no personal relationship.

You don't have to destroy or neglect your relationships with family and friends to serve God in ministry. You don't have to lose your kids to be "on fire" for God or to be effective in the marketplace. In fact, we will see that God uses the maturity that is cultivated when you build relationships with those close to you as a platform so you can effectively deal with situations beyond family and friends.

Since that day in '82, the Bible has become a new book for me. It seems as I open the pages, I discover afresh the revelation of the value that God places on our relationships with one another. We do not have to wander in neglect, misunderstanding, unforgiveness, bitterness, hurt, or regret like "shell-shocked" veterans returning from the relational battlefield when it comes to getting along. God's Word packs wisdom that will bring peace and joy into every human relationship.

In the next chapter we'll look at *why* God says relationships are so important.

2

THE IMPORTANCE OF RELATIONSHIPS

Throughout the first two chapters of Genesis, you find the phrase "and God saw that it was good" used repeatedly. That was God's reply as He reflected on each aspect of the creation He had made. Genesis 1:31 says, "God saw all that he had made, and it was **very good**." Yet, after these declarations concerning His creation God says something very different in relation to man. In Genesis 2:18 He looks at man and says, "It is not good . . .". He wasn't saying that **man** wasn't good (be nice, ladies!), but that the *situation* he was in wasn't good.

That brings up an interesting theological question. Why did God create a situation that was not good?! The situation He was speaking of was that man was **alone!** "The LORD God said, 'It is not good for the man **to be alone**. I will make a helper suitable for him.'" (Genesis 2:18)

God is making a profound statement in this verse. He is saying that He created man to need more than just a relationship with God! He created us to **need each other.** It wasn't that God was lacking or not able to be all we needed, but that He *designed* us to need each other ─ I call it the *dependency factor.*

Interestingly, God did not create Eve immediately after identifying man's need. After saying, "I will make him a helper" in verse 18, you would have expected God to create Eve without delay. But that did not happen until verse 22, "And the Lord God fashioned into a woman the rib which He had taken from the man, and brought her to the man." Instead, He started bringing *animals* around for Adam to name. "And out of the ground the Lord God formed every beast of the field and every bird of the sky, and brought them to the man to see what he would call them; and whatever the man called a living creature, that was its name. And the man gave names to all the cattle, and to the birds of the sky, and to every beast of the field, but for Adam there was not found a helper suitable for him." (Vs. 19-20)

At first glance, it seems that God forgot that He said He was going to make Adam a helper. Why would He start bringing animals around instead of creating Eve right away?

But God did not forget what He was doing ─ He had a problem. He knew what Adam needed, but Adam didn't. So, God brought the animals before Adam to make him *aware* of his need. As Adam began to name them, he began to realize that all the animals had others like them but he had no one like himself.

With this strategy, God was able to alert Adam to his need as well as establish the fact in Adam's mind that nothing on this planet could meet that need except *another person*.

If Eve would have shown up before Adam knew he needed her, I'm convinced his male ego would have driven him to "mark off" the garden so *his* territory was obvious to the intruder!

It wasn't until verse 21, after Adam was aware of his need, that God created Eve. "So the Lord God caused a deep sleep to fall upon the man, and he slept; then He took one of his ribs, and closed up the flesh at that place."

Notice that God did not go back to the dust of the earth to create Eve. He took what He needed out of Adam's side without replacing what He took, and then He fashioned Eve. When Adam awoke, part of him was missing. Part of his spiritual, emotional, and physiological makeup was gone — and he sensed it! He was now even more incomplete and alone! God was building the *dependency factor*.

When God finally brought Eve to him, he exclaimed, "This is now bone of my bones, and flesh of my flesh; you're part of me! You shall be called woman because you were taken out of man, out of me!" (V. 23 — Author's Paraphrase)

Most think that needing others, or having to depend upon others, is a sign of weakness. Our society teaches us that independence equals strength, when just the opposite is true. It takes great strength to get along with others. You have to have a lot of intestinal fortitude and plain ol' guts to stay in relationships, trust God to help you, and negotiate your differences. All it takes is a well developed attitude of selfishness to run out and do your own thing. There is an abundance of that these days.

God created us with a need for others. The need for meaningful relationships **was not** a result of man's fall into sin. The *dependency factor* of creation was the plan and will of God. We were designed to need each other *before the Fall!* In fact, we fulfill God's created order when we recognize that need.

By sharing this I am not encouraging smothering, *co-dependent* relationships. People who have been abused or abandoned by others often carry the pain of old relationships into new ones. They often try to get people in new relationships to make-up for all the evil that has been done to them previously. They are like a lamprey-eel that sucks all the life out of its prey. True dependence on others is not a devouring, deleterious, suffocating thing. It is a mutually supportive expression of created order.

People who have been hurt need to learn how to forgive those who have offended them in the past so that they do not poison their future relationships with the pain of past ones. We'll talk about forgiveness later.

Why God Created Us With the Dependency Factor

Try to look at creation from God's perspective. He has created this wonderful being called man. As the crown of His creation, He created him with will and intellect. He created man with the capacity of choice because He did not want to force man into serving Him. He wanted man to have the free choice whether or not to walk with God. But how is God supposed to let this man know how He feels about him? In those first days of reaching out to His creation, how can He communicate His love for Adam or tell him of the plans, dreams, and purposes He has for him?

For God to tell him, "I love you," would have meant as much as saying "I *glamba* you." How could Adam understand love? For God to say "I long for your fellowship," would have meant nothing to him! That is the reason God **gave man** the capacity to love and to need others. **This capacity enables us to understand how God feels toward us!**

The Apostle Paul said in Ephesians 1:17, "I keep asking that the God of our Lord Jesus Christ, the glorious Father, may give you the Spirit of wisdom and revelation, so that you may **know him better**." Near the end of Paul's life, he still writes, "I want to **know Christ**. . .". Philippians 3:10 Anything that can help us "know Him" better is of paramount importance.

Paul said in Ephesians 5:31-32, "For this reason a man will leave his father and mother and be united to his wife, and the two will become one flesh. This is a profound mystery —— **but I am talking about Christ and the church**." *Marriage speaks of the relationship between God and man!* In other words, something in the relationship between a man and woman as husband and wife gives us a "snapshot" of what God feels toward us. Marriage was created to help us understand God.

The Parable of Parenthood

The same is true of parenthood. When a woman becomes a mother she gets to view life from a whole new perspective. The baby is conceived as the result of love for her husband. Her body houses the precious life growing inside her. Then she lays her life on the line while birthing the child. As she places her new baby on her breasts to nourish and care for it, gazing into that innocent face, something happens inside her. *In that moment* she captures a glimpse of what God feels like when He looks at us! God said in Isaiah 49:15,

> "Can a mother forget the baby at her breast and have no compassion on the child she has borne? Though she may forget, I will not forget you!"

Then He said, "As a mother comforts her child, so will I comfort you." (Isaiah 66:13)

Where did natural fathers get the capacity to love and care for their children? "For this reason I kneel before **the Father**, from whom his whole family **in heaven and on earth** derives its name." (Ephesians 3:14-15) In other words, the only reason we have the capacity for fatherhood and family on earth is because God gave us that capacity! He did it to reveal a portion of His nature to us — to show us His heart. God did not watch mankind evolve into families and then call Himself "Father" and heaven "home" to relate to us. He was always *Father*. Heaven was always *home*. He gave us the capacity to have homes so that *we* could better relate to *Him*! Jesus uses the parenting example to explain what God is like in Matthew 7:11:

> "If you, then, though you are evil, know how to give good gifts to your children, how much more will your Father in heaven give good gifts to those who ask him!"

Over the past 20 years I have ministered to thousands of people. I have discovered that most people tend to view God as they do their parents — especially their fathers. If their dad was always around and giving, they have very little difficulty seeing God that way. If their dad was always gone or very uninvolved in their lives, they have to battle with feelings of being left alone and forsaken by God. If Dad was very demanding, corrective and strict, they feel that God is constantly angry with them and disappointed in them.

When the prophet Samuel first heard the voice of God in 1 Samuel chapter three, he thought it was the voice of his authority figure, Eli.

"The LORD called Samuel a third time, and Samuel got up and went to Eli and said, 'Here I am; you called me.' Then Eli realized that the LORD was calling the boy. So Eli told Samuel, 'Go and lie down, and if he calls you, say, 'Speak, LORD, for your servant is listening." So Samuel went and lay down in his place. The LORD came and stood there, calling as at the other times, 'Samuel! Samuel!' Then Samuel said, 'Speak, for your servant is listening.'" (vs. 8-10)

This story shows us that the place a parent holds in the life of a young child is the place that God will eventually hold in that child. Because of our position as parents, we must avoid being destructive in the lives of our children. If a parent is representing the devil more than God, the child's capacity to understand God will be greatly impaired.

That is why Jesus spoke so sternly about being destructive in children's lives.

"If anyone should cause one of these little ones to lose faith in me, it would be better for that person to have a large millstone tied around his neck and be drowned in the deep sea. How terrible for the world that there are things that make people lose their faith! Such things will always happen — but how terrible for the one who causes them!" (Matthew 18:6-7 GNB)

This verse applies to parents more than to any other group of people.

The good news is that when parents fail miserably God can still make up for the loss. He will build into our lives what our parents should have. Psalms 68:5 says that God is "a father to the fatherless." Because no human parent is perfect, everyone of us need God to parent us to one degree or another.

My Dad is a physician and wasn't around the house that much while I was growing up. He was loving and kind to us, but seldom had time to be involved in the details of our lives. It took me a while to realize it, but my relationship with God had taken on some traits of my relationship with my Dad! Because of the love and kindness that both he and my Mom showed me, I could easily sense God's love for me. But there was a hindering aspect as well. I discovered that my difficulty believing that God was interested in my everyday life was hinged to my Dad. I knew God loved me. I knew He wanted to provide for me. But I couldn't believe He wanted to walk with me and be an intimate part of my day because I never experienced that with my dad.

Though God does reveal Himself to us through relationships, God's **primary** method of revelation is by the personal work of the Holy Spirit through the Scriptures. Your relationship with God does not have to be limited to how good or bad your parents were! It took some time, but through the Scriptures God built a new, clearer image of Himself in my heart. The Lord led me to verses that revealed that He was with me and interested in my life. My faith soared as I got to know the God of the Bible. You can't really know God by how you feel. You can't trust what you know about Him by what you have experienced. Clarity comes when you read what He says about Himself in the Bible. However, parenting does provide some revelation of God and should be taken seriously.

The Parables of Brothers, Sisters, and Friendships

What about sibling relationships? "We who have been made holy by Jesus, now have the same Father he has. That is why Jesus is not ashamed to call us **his brothers**." (Hebrews 2:11 TLB) The way brothers and sisters feel about each other is a gift from God to help us further understand how He feels about us.

Even our capacity and desire for friendships answer to God's plan of revealing Himself to us. Jesus said, "Greater love has no one than this, that he lay down his life for his friends. **You are my friends**." (John 15:13)

Every human relationship we have in some way gives us a glimpse of God's care and love for us. They are "parables" that reveal God's heart for His creation. I don't think it is a coincidence that Jesus spent thirty years of His life learning how to relate to others around Him. At age 12 He felt ready to go into ministry. His parents found Him preaching and asking questions in the temple. But Jesus was quick to honor His relationship with His parents when His mother told Him to come home.

God in His wisdom designed the home and our friendships to be *parables* that reveal His nature. It seems as we work out our differences and get in each other's faces every day, something happens within us that enables us to understand God better and prepares us to accomplish God's perfect will for our lives.

Though relationships are **not** God's primary method of revealing Himself, they do speak of Him. If perverted, they will hinder a person's life and capacity for faith! In over 90 percent of the counseling situations I have been involved with, the problem had its root, at least in part, in some sort of relational dysfunction. That is why Satan gets involved here!

Why do you think Satan never even approached man until **after there was a relationship**? (See Genesis 2-3) The first evidence of the Fall was Adam pointing the finger of blame at Eve, and then at God. The first murder was between two brothers. Relational dysfunction is one of Satan's master deceptions.

Satan knows that if he can destroy our capacity to relate, he has destroyed one of God's methods of revealing His nature to the human race. If he can turn a marriage from being a refuge of peace and security into being a place of tyranny and destruction, where it can no longer "speak concerning Christ and the Church" — then he has dealt an effective blow to the kingdom of God.

Next, let's look at the power inherent in relationships.

And now nothing which they purpose to do
will be impossible for them.

Ge 11:6

3

THE POWER OF RELATIONSHIPS

The potential for greatness in our lives is not found in discovering new ways to isolate and insulate ourselves, but in tapping into the power that flows when we begin to unify with those around us. Look at what God said about the people building the tower of Babel in Genesis 11:5-6: "And the Lord said, 'Behold, they are **one people**, and they all have the same language. And this is what they began to do, and now **nothing which they purpose to do will be impossible for them.**'"

The King James version reads, "And now nothing will be restrained from them, which they have imagined to do." (Genesis 11:6)

When these individuals entered a *unified relationship*, they increased their power to such a degree that God declared they could accomplish *any* task. God does not exaggerate! He is saying that unity greatly increases the potential for accomplishment.

The people at Babel failed because they pursued *their will* and not the will of God. God, in turn, intervened and scrambled their communications.

What can we learn from this? First, that we can accomplish more together than we can on our own. Healthy relationships increase our ability to achieve purposes and goals. Secondly, if we find the will of God on a matter and get someone to agree with us, we are well on the way to success.

Every church should experience this unity! Jesus promised that we could shake the world if we would place enough value on our relationships with each other to get into unity. "That they may **all be one**; even as Thou, Father, art in Me, and I in Thee, that they also may be in Us; **that the world may believe** that Thou didst send Me." (John 17:21)

Unity Strengthens Prayer

Concerning our prayer life, Jesus says, "Again I say to you, that if two of you agree on earth about anything that they may ask, it shall be done for them by My Father who is in heaven. For where two or three have **gathered together** in My name, there I am in their midst." (Matthew 18:19-20) When we join our hearts together it increases our prayer power.

Unity Brings the Supernatural

Whenever the supernatural appears in the book of Acts, phrases pop up that reveal the presence of unity. "And when the day of Pentecost had fully come, **they were all with one accord** in **one place**. And suddenly there came a sound from heaven as of a rushing mighty wind, and it filled all the house where they were sitting." (Acts 2:1-2 KJV)

> "And the congregation of those who believed were of **one heart and soul**; and not one of them claimed that anything belonging to him was his own; but all things were common property to them. And **with great power** the apostles were giving witness to the resurrection of the Lord Jesus, and abundant grace was upon them all." (Acts 4:32-33)

There is something precious and powerful about our choice to care for and open ourselves up to each other. There is a flow of God's life that builds and restores us and brings the supernatural release of God's power.

Unity is a Command

Because of its impact, unity is a command. The Epistles urge us repeatedly to strive for unity in our relationships. (viz. Philippians 2:1-3, Ephesians 4:2-3, 31-32) When we do not value our relationships and we allow them to deteriorate without striving for their success, the result is a shut-down of spiritual power in our lives.

Disunity Grieves the Holy Spirit

Ephesians 4:30 reads, "And do not **grieve** the Holy Spirit of God, by whom you were sealed for the day of redemption." We know that this *grieving* is over relational conflict because this verse is sandwiched between two others that deal with our relationships with one another.

Disunity Hinders Prayer

The following verses show us how broken relationships hinder prayer.

"Therefore I say to you, all things for which you pray and ask, believe that you have received them, and they shall be granted you. And whenever you stand praying, forgive, **if you have anything against anyone**; so that your Father also who is in heaven may forgive you your transgressions. But if you do not forgive, neither will your Father who is in heaven forgive your transgressions." (Mark 11:24-26)

"You husbands likewise, live with your wives in an understanding way, as with a weaker vessel, since she is a woman; and grant her honor as a fellow heir of the grace of life, so **that your prayers may not be hindered**." (I Peter 3:7)

Satan's Playground

Satan knows the power that accompanies *unified relationships*. He knows the spiritual breakdown that occurs in the life of the believer when relational tension goes unresolved. So, Satan attacks us in this vital area.

Remember that Satan was once a ruling angel. He does not want any human being to have spiritual power because that would hinder his ability to control and dominate them. He knows that unity brings power. One reason God is all-powerful is because Father, Son and Holy Spirit are ONE. If we walk in unity with God and with each other, Satan knows he would have no place in our lives. **Relationships threaten the kingdom of darkness!**

Remember that Satan did not try to approach man in Genesis until after there was a relationship. ". . . and **they** (Adam and Eve) **shall become one** . . . **Now the serpent** . . .". (Genesis 2:24; 3:1) The serpent is still trying to infiltrate our lives today, trying to get us into disunity with each other and God!

In Ephesians chapters 4-6, God sets forth how we are to deal with relationships between the saints. He discusses the relationship of ministers with the Body of Christ (4:11-16); the relationship we have with God as worshippers (5:19-20); the relationship we have as helpers in the church (5:21); the home relationships of wife and husband and child and parent (5:22-6:4); and the relationship between employee and employer (6:4-9).

As Paul closes his discourse, he shares about spiritual warfare starting in verse 10. It is here we discover that Satan's key strategy against us deals with relationships. "Finally, be strong in the Lord, and in the strength of His might. Put on the full armor of God that you may be able to stand firm against the schemes of the devil." (V. 11)

Notice the tension of these verses. Paul is getting serious here!

35

He is telling us to take on God's strength and might and to put on His *full* armor. This is tantamount to the President of the United States putting our armed forces on full alert!

What is up? What devious scheme is the enemy plotting here? Is there cancer on the horizon? Maybe a past due bill? Perhaps I won't get that promotion I've been longing for after all!?! But that is not what's happening here.

Satan's scheme unfolds in the next verse, "For our struggle is not against **flesh and blood**, but against the rulers, against the powers, against the world forces of this darkness, against the spiritual forces of wickedness in the heavenly places." (V. 12)

Satan's scheme is to get you and me to think that the struggles we have in our lives are the direct result of **flesh and blood** — the people with whom we are in relationship. He wants you and me to get into *disunity*. He knows that if we do, we will grieve the Holy Spirit and cripple the effectiveness of our prayers.

For years, I thought the schemes of the devil dealt only with outward things like tragedy, sickness, lack, etc. Those things are from Satan, but did you ever wonder *why* he uses those things? Does he just want us sick just for sickness' sake, or is sickness just one weapon he uses to carry out his *real* strategy? I believe His scheme is to destroy our relationships with others and especially the one we have *with God*!

Think about it. When you are sick, you tend to think of no one but yourself. Satan loves that because *selfishness* is a seed of destruction for any relationship. You are weakened through sickness and others must care for you. They must also take on the responsibilities you would normally handle. Sickness can strain a relationship to the point of *disunity*. Then if healing is not forthcoming, you may even begin to question God's attitude and faithfulness toward you, potentially straining your relationship with Him!

The same is true in times of financial pressure. The lack itself is only part of Satan's plan. His real plan is to use the pressure caused by financial and material lack to strain our relationships to the breaking point. Financial pressure is a major cause of divorce.

Satan uses pressures like these to attack our marriages, homes, friendships and even our faith in God! The forces of darkness would love for you to think that the source of your problems is your pastor, your boss, your parents, your co-workers, your spouse, your kids, and ultimately, God. Satan knows that any un-ironed wrinkle in a relationship means spiritual paralysis for you.

He knows what unforgiveness does. He knows how it evolves into bitterness that "springs up" and "causes trouble," "and by it many be defiled," according to Hebrews 12:15.

Do you realize there are many believers today who are walking around defiled, lacking power with God, having unnecessary trouble in their lives simply because they are nursing a *grudge*?

Verses like Matthew 6:14-15 clearly show that it does not pay to hold grudges.

"For if you forgive men for their transgressions, your heavenly Father will also forgive you. But if you do not forgive men, then your Father **will not** forgive your transgressions."

Unforgiveness severely impairs your spiritual perception and keeps you from discerning how to cooperate with God in your life. In Acts 8 we see Simon the Sorcerer offering money to buy the power of the Holy Spirit. Peter rebukes him saying, "I see that you are **full of bitterness** and captive to sin."

Because of Simon's bitterness He was unable to participate in what God was doing. It also caused him to distort what was going on. This happens to us whenever we embrace bitterness. We lose a clear perspective of our lives and spiritual reality.

Satan knows these things. His strategy is to get you offended, then into unforgiveness, then finally into bitterness. Trouble will then spring up everywhere in your life and your relationships with God and man will die.

Paul is warning us in Ephesians 6. Let me paraphrase what he is saying: "Watch out! You're going to need every bit of God's power you can grasp to make it in the evil day, when offense is nigh thee! The enemy will try to convince you that *people* are making life hard on you. *'Your spouse (or pastor, or boss) is picking on you and holding you back.'* Satan will say, *'You're wonderful. Others are just too controlling and selfish to see it.'* But don't listen to the devil! Instead, put on all God's armor or you'll get bamboozled by Satan's lies and get embittered at people and lose out with God!"

Satan wants us to think our struggle is against **flesh and blood**. He wants pastors to hate parishioners, workers to despise their bosses, spouses to think they married the wrong person, children to rebel against their parents, and so on. He wants us to think our problem is the people around us so that we are always in the "defense mode" —— self-preserving, self-defending and self-protecting.

He wants us to feel it's just better to stick to yourself . . . you don't get hurt then. He wants us to violate our *dependency factor* so we are alienated from other people and in disobedience to God.

Don't be duped by hell! The forces of darkness are behind relational conflict. When it arises, do as God did when He encountered man's first relational conflict with Himself. "And the Lord God said to the serpent, 'Because you have done this, **cursed are you** more than all cattle, and more than every beast of the field; on your belly shall you go and dust shall you eat all the days of your life.'"

When trouble comes, take authority over Satan. Command him to flee. The Bible says, "Resist the devil and he will flee," and "Give no place to the devil." Command Satan to get on the ground and then tread on him (Luke 10:19). With him out of the way, we can take the steps necessary to resolve the relational tensions that arise in our relationships with each other.

God loves us the way we are,
  but he loves us too much to leave us that way.

Leighton Ford

4

LET'S RE-EVALUATE

The Bible stresses two central themes — man's relationship with God, and man's relationship with his fellowman. From beginning to end, we are constantly urged to keep those relationships right.

The psalmist refers to a special "blessing" from God that comes when we place value on walking in right relationship with those in our world.

"Behold, how good and how pleasant it is for brothers to dwell together in unity! . . . For there the Lord commanded **the blessing** — life forever." (Psalm 133:1, 3)

In the New Testament Jesus says, "A new commandment I give

to you, that you love one another, even as I have loved you, that you also love one another." (John 13:34) The Apostle Paul picks up on the theme and says, "If possible, so far as it depends on you, be at peace with all men." (Romans 12:18)

These verses show us that how we deal with others is important to God. He wants us to have healthy relationships and He reserves a blessing for those who decide to cultivate them. As we learn to depend on each other, a strength and power come that we could never have gained on our own.

Sadly, we don't often see things like God does. Consequently, many place little value on their relationships and even tend to take those closest to them for granted.

Why We Take Each Other For Granted

Because we don't honor each other as God intended, we take each other for granted and end up *possessing* one another. Whatever we possess has a way of disappearing. Let me give you an example.

Some years back, my wife and I purchased an abandoned home that needed much renovation. One of our major projects was replacing the 30-year old, harvest-colored, shag carpeting that was disgustingly filthy. We had pulled the carpet out and hoped the new one would be put in before our moving day.

As it turned out, the carpet was delayed and we moved into the home with the old carpet nails precariously sticking out of the floor along with the remaining toe-jam-like carpet pad webbed between the nails

Our second son, Robert, was about 6 months old at the time and was an avid crawler and escape artist. Gail grieved as she

42

would catch him crawling on the old nails, pausing to eat the carpet remains. It was awful. After about two weeks of this, the carpet man came. We sang a refrain of *This is the Day That the Lord has Made.*

I left early that morning as they began to prep the floor for the carpet. When I returned in a couple of hours, they hadn't yet rolled out the carpet, but just the foam base they had laid seemed impressive. When I arrived that evening, most of the carpet had been laid. It was gorgeous. The nap seemed four feet high. It was as if the carpet were singing to me, "Here I am; I've finally arrived." I checked it out from every angle. The next morning I leaned over the stair rail and rechecked it. It was so different and new and beautiful that it gripped me.

In the days that followed, I would stop and admire our new carpet as I came into the house. But slowly it began to lose my interest — it was becoming mine. I finally *possessed* it and it's power to grab me disappeared. Now and then, visitors would comment on the carpet, and I would remember glimpses of how it first affected me, but that time had passed.

We tend to do that with one another — especially with those close to us (spouses, children, fellow workers, etc.). *Possessing* people robs them of the specialness and value. They "disappear" because we cease to give them a special place in our lives. They lose their ability to "wow" or to "grip" us. That seems to give us license for thoughtlessness, inconsiderate behavior, and even rudeness.

People of Productivity?

Because we don't value people the way God calls us to, our work or ministry often takes a higher priority than it should. Our work ethic is so deeply imprinted upon us, that we see time spent on anything other than work or ministry as wasteful and unproductive.

Many are like I used to be, viewing God's will as only relating to work and productivity. So they place little value on their relationships, seeing those relationships as potential hindrances to doing the work they were created to do.

I believe God destines us to do specific things in business and ministry; "For we are His workmanship, created in Christ Jesus for **good works**, which God prepared beforehand, that we should walk in them." (Ephesians 2:10) But are activity and accomplishment really God's *only* area of concern? If you think they are, you will run full speed ahead, viewing people as expendable resources that you either use or ignore. If you believe relationships with people are equally important, you will be sensitive and try to involve loved ones in areas to which you feel God has called you, whether business or ministry.

Jesus showed us that close *personal relationships* actually take priority over *accomplishment*. As a boy, He told His parents that He had to be about His "Father's business," but He quickly submitted to Mom and Dad when they told Him to come home. Jesus placed value on maintaining successful relationships even when it meant postponing the specific accomplishments He knew God the Father had destined for Him to do.

The reason Jesus placed such value on relationships is that the GENERAL will of God for Jesus to get along with those close to Him took precedence over the SPECIFIC will of God, which dealt with accomplishment. I am convinced that obeying the GENERAL will of God concerning getting along with others *prepared* Jesus for obeying the SPECIFIC will for His public ministry and passion on the cross! This principle holds true for us as well.

It wasn't until the age of thirty that Jesus began to follow more SPECIFIC revelations from God for His life. Why do we want to take shortcuts in God's will for us? Maybe we do because it is more difficult to "get along" with people in our world than it is to "do" things for them.

Shortcuts may appeal to us because we can do more, and get further ahead *personally*, when we don't have to service relationships! Relationships take away time that we could have devoted to furthering career or ministry, resulting in greater personal productivity.

That is why Paul encouraged young men and women to remain single if they could. "Yet I wish that all men were even as I myself am." (I Corinthians 7:8) He was referring to his singleness. Jesus said there would be a day when men would choose celibacy "for the sake of the Kingdom of Heaven" (Matthew 19:12). There are people who want to take on life-consuming Gospel projects. Notice that the Bible encourages these folks to choose non-marriage if they are going to be extremely involved with "doing." Paul shows that the marriage relationship has priority over ministry when he says, "The one who is married is concerned about the things of the world, how he may please his wife, and **his interests are divided** . . . and the [woman] who is married is concerned about the things of this world, how she may please her husband." (I Corinthians 7:33-34) Once you have made the choice to marry and have a family, you must take the time to nourish those relationships.

The problem comes when we choose to be in relationships but

don't want to work on them for their success. Many want the benefits of having a spouse and children but don't want to have any inconvenience because of them. As the old saying goes, "You can't have your cake and eat it too!"

I'm not suggesting that you can't do great things after marrying and having a family. There is good news for those of us engaged in committed human relationships! Though we may not reach as many *personal* goals when we increase our sphere of relationships through marriage and family, we will ultimately make a greater impact on our world as we pour ourselves into others. The difference will be that many of our accomplishments will be achieved *with and through others.*

This is a difficult concept for us to grasp, but our lives have the greatest total impact when we back off from personal accomplishment and pour ourselves into others. Through our dealings with others we strengthen *them* to accomplish more. But doing things with and through others is usually not as exciting as doing things yourself. It is more difficult to grasp a sense of personal worth and value over what you have done with others versus what you could have done alone.

We Need Vision
It is obviously more glamorous to traverse the planet preaching in major conventions or landing "big deals" as a successful businessman than it is to make sure you have the extra time to take your bride out on dates and to play mini-golf with your kids. Yet, God's will for most men and women is for them to be deeply involved with nourishing and developing intimate relationships. God **does not** want most of us to be "famous" and doing what is

"great" in the eyes of men. God isn't trying to cramp your style —
He just knows how you can best impact your world.

You and I may *reason* that doing important things in the eyes
of men is the only way to fulfill God's destiny for our lives, but that
does not mean God thinks that way. Isaiah 55:8 says, "'For My
thoughts are not your thoughts, neither are your ways My ways,'
declares the Lord."

Focusing on helping others at the expense of personal goals and
dreams is God's will for most of us! "Do not merely look out for
your own personal interests, but also for the interests of others."
(Philippians 2:4)

God chose Abraham because He knew Abraham would spend
time developing others at the expense of not experiencing self-
accomplishment. "For I have chosen him, in order that **he may
command his children and his household after him** to keep
the way of the Lord by doing righteousness and justice; in order
that the Lord may bring upon Abraham what He has spoken about
him." (Genesis 18:19)

Some of us have to rid ourselves of the mentality that the only
activity that really counts is what we do *personally*. We must be
men and women of vision. We must see beyond the obvious and
realize that spending ourselves to secure healthy, successful
relationships with family and friends will ultimately produce
dramatic results.

The Scriptures say of Abraham, "By faith Abraham, when he
was called, obeyed by going out to a place which he was to receive
for an inheritance; and he went out, not knowing where he was
going." (Hebrews 11:8) Later in the same chapter it speaks of
Abraham and some others, "All these died in faith, **without
receiving the promises**." (V. 13)

47

Think of it. Abraham did not get to inhabit the land he set out to possess. His role was to pour himself into his children and they were the ones who would see the fulfillment of that promise. Abraham fulfilled God's ultimate plan *through* others.

In Psalm 127, God speaks of our children as "gifts of the Lord." He says, "Like arrows in the hand of a warrior, so are the children of one's youth. How blessed is the man whose quiver is full of them; **they shall not be ashamed**."

You may feel like you are wasting your time by spending it with your children; but when you build secure, balanced, strong children and give them memories that undergird their lives, you make yourself a "warrior" and they become "arrows" that go further than you could have ever gone on your own! When you value this, you will stand before God and "not be ashamed" because you chose not to do more spectacular things personally.

The following is an example of a father who did not see the value of spending time with his son.

"Brook Adams kept a diary from his boyhood. One special day, when he was eight years old he wrote in his diary: 'Went fishing with my Dad, the most glorious day of my life.'

"Throughout the next 40 years of his life he kept a diary and he never forgot that day he went fishing with his father and through the diary he makes repeated references commenting on the influence that this day had in his life.

"Brook's father was an important man — he was Charles Francis Adams, the U.S. Ambassador to Great Britain under the Lincoln Administration. Interestingly, he too made a note in his diary about that fishing trip. This is what he wrote: 'Went fishing with my son, a day wasted.'"[1]

A *single* day spent with his father became a springboard of inspiration for young Adams' life. What more could he have done, or been, if Dad would have invested more?

In her book, *Marriage to a Difficult Man*, Elizabeth Dodds shows how a mother's influence can continue to impact the world for generations after she has gone. The book reveals the achievements and contributions of the descendants of Sarah Edwards, wife of the famous eighteenth-century preacher Jonathan Edwards. From the eleven children and their offspring the family produced:

-13 college presidents
-65 professors
-100 lawyers and a dean of a law school
-30 judges
-66 physicians and a dean of a medical school
-80 public office holders, including

    3 mayors
    3 governors
    3 United States senators
    a controller of the United States treasury
    a vice-president of the United States.

Chances are Sarah Edwards was unable to foresee all this as she fed, clothed and invested her love and values into her children. She probably felt that she was doing little for the world while mothering them in the "daily grind" of life — unless she was looking at what she was doing with eyes of faith.

God takes this business of parenting very seriously. The prophet Eli brought severe judgment to his family because he refused to take his job as a father seriously. His life's work was actually destroyed! "I will put an end to your family, so that it will no longer serve as priests. Every member will die before his time. None shall live to be old. You will envy the prosperity I will give my people, but you and your family will be in distress and need. Not one of them will live out his days. Those who are left alive will live in sadness and grief; and their children shall die by the sword." (1 Samuel 2:31-33 TLB)

You don't *have* to take *every* business opportunity. You don't have to take *every* opportunity to minister to outsiders. The balance is found in doing what you can, but making sure your "doing" does not breed neglect and tension in the home. If tension comes, attend to it. **Tension demands attention!** It takes time, flexibility, and a dependence upon the Holy Spirit to keep this in check.

I believe that there are special callings for people to do unusual things —— things that are glamorous and weighty in the eyes of man; but God's highest call is for us to get along with Him and others and to face life without burning out, with a wonderful balance between ministry, work, rest, and recreation.

Paul said by the Holy Spirit, "Make it your ambition to lead a quiet life and attend to your own business and work with your own hands, just as we commanded you." (I Thessalonians 2:11)

Richard Exley says so brilliantly, "When was the last time you recall someone getting a 'pat on the back' for 'taking it easy' and 'keeping his priorities' in check as this verse suggests? We admire and honor extremists."[2]

The Importance of Everyday Living

Every member of the Body of Christ would delight in their daily lives if they understood the kind of value God places on the ordinary.

Jesus was born in a manger —— you can't get more ordinary than that. He grew up in a small village and learned how to be a carpenter. He could have introduced nuclear physics. He could have built the first airplane. He could have been the father of the industrial revolution.

Yet, He spent thirty years being ordinary. He dealt with career choices. He was the head of His home after Joseph died (most scholars agree that His father must have died shortly after Jesus was 12 years of age). He dealt with advertising, customers, organization, and growing in God, all at the same time.

Why did He choose the ordinary? You can't find a better school of the Spirit than the home and marketplace. It is there that the Word of God leaves the realm of theology and enters the realm of practicality. If you can live out what you believe in front of those closest to you, you will not only *do* great things for God —— you will *be* great for God.

Jesus involved himself in the lives of His brothers and sisters as they grew. He grew up watching the traveling merchants buy and sell. He saw the sowers sowing by hand in their fields. These stories from everyday life formed the vignettes through which He brought His life-changing message to earth.

Think about this . . . God valued the ordinary enough to spend all but three of His years on this planet *experiencing it* before doing the actual work He was destined to do.

Did I Miss Something?

I have been in the Body of Christ for almost twenty years and have heard thousands of sermons by a host of ministers. I may have missed something, but I don't recall many ministers relating how to apply my faith to ordinary living or within the context of our relationships with one another. The main focus of the teaching I have heard has been on doing something great or spectacular for God.

I have heard ministers preach on God's ability to open doors for those who trusted him and then they would share stories of how God opened doors for them. They had wonderful stories of visiting kings, winning 10,000 people to Christ in an open air meeting in a foreign land, of someone donating $50,000 for a printing press that was needed in their Philippine office, etc. God had really opened doors for them!

But as I sat in the auditorium I thought, "I've never met a king — not even my state representative. I'd be afraid to talk to 10,000 people in a foreign land all at once; and I don't have an outreach in the Philippines, so I don't need a press. I guess God won't open doors for me!?"

I was left with a longing to *do* something great for God. It is precisely this focus on *accomplishment* that causes the American church to devalue their everyday lives and relationships with others.

Sadly, the only relational teachings I heard were from Christian psychologists, not ministers. In fact, those trained in ministry have often received little or no training in this vital area. Consequently, many in ministry have *lost* their children and marriages while they were trying to *find* the "lost sheep" of the world.

Building relationships may not seem as important to us as

winning thousands to Christ or earning millions of dollars, but God thinks it is! Maybe God sees things a little differently than we do. When we do things His way, maybe we end up touching the world after all. Maybe it is true that when a husband treats a wife the way the Bible commands that our marriages touch others beyond what we see. Maybe we end up, as the Scriptures promise, to be "speaking in reference to Christ and the Church" (Ephesians 5:32) as a living testimony to the world!

The non-Christian may have a difficult time relating to a tract or to one of our church services, but relationships speak a universal language they will understand. Our marriages speak of Christ and the Church. Our relationships with our children speak of the Father God and His family. If we will let God fill our relational lives, we will capture the attention of a dying, lonely world. Then we can "**give an account** for the hope that is in us." (1 Peter 3:15)

"Husbands love your wives." "Let the wife see to it that she respect her husband." These are not class "B" Bible verses, secondary to class "A" action verses like, "Go into all the world and preach the gospel to all creation."

For years as a pastor I have preached on the value of the home and marriage as one of God's primary methods of evangelization. I have seen family after family drawn to our church because they have seen the stability and love of the married couples and family units within our church. Many of our couples have been married for years and are still mistaken for newlyweds. We began valuing what God values and it accomplished things beyond what we imagined. I believe God knows what He is doing when He asks us to do things. If we cooperate with Him we will fulfill our destiny!

We need to re-evaluate! The "work of the Lord" is not just running around the world trying to reach people we do not know at the expense of losing touch with the people God has already placed in our lives. Although we are called to reach out, we must remember that those closest to us are important as well.

We are doing the will of God when we love our spouses, train our children, care for our parents, and nourish our friendships. The relationships we already have matter to God.

Many things God calls us to do may seem a waste of time and energy, yet they are the ways God has chosen to enable us to really impact our world. How many times have you been praying and felt you were making *little* headway. Yet, you stuck in there! Why? Because you know that prayer is important in the long haul. You know that something happens in you and in the world when you pray. You may not see immediate results, but you know that it is important to keep on keepin' on. We must trust that Jesus knows what He is doing when He commands us to do something. After all, He is the one who heads the church, longs for the lost to be saved, and shepherds our lives.

If relationships are so important, how do we effectively deal with conflict so that they are not destroyed? We'll look at that next.

Together we stick, divided we're stuck.
            Evon Hedley

5

THE GROUNDS FOR RESOLVING CONFLICT

When you first meet someone there is a natural strength within us to want to communicate, share, give and forbear with that person. But after you are around them for any length of time, you begin to identify things about them that bother you. After getting past being bothered, we often get hurt by what they do or say. Once we are hurt we try to pull back from the relationship because we no longer have the strength to continue communicating, sharing, giving, and forbearing with that person.

Those who *claim* they don't want to get involved in relationships do so because they have been hurt or have had some negative relational experiences in their past. But we don't function well alone because we were created to need others. We humans are strange birds. We need each other and yet, after we get familiar, we can't stand each other.

We must learn to deal with relational conflict once it comes. But how?

Just like most things we face in our lives, there is a *natural human* response, and then there is the *Christian* response.

From a *natural* standpoint, when an incident occurs that brings conflict, we immediately want two things to happen. First, we want to identify the "guilty" party (unless it is us!). Secondly, we want to find a way to "get even" or make the person pay in some way for what was done. Let's take a closer look at both of these *natural* responses.

Who is Guilty?

In most cases identifying the guilty party is pretty difficult to do because it usually takes two to tango! In almost every conflict both parties are right *and* wrong in various degrees. The problem is that our human nature usually overlooks what wrong we may have done and then places the spotlight on what we perceive to be the *unthinkable* actions of the other person.

Blaming others for our relational conflict began the moment Satan got involved with the human race. When God asked Adam and Eve to explain why they ate of the forbidden tree, they immediately began to deny responsibility.

"And He (God) said, 'Who told you that you were naked? Have you eaten from the tree of which I commanded you not to eat?' And the man said, '**The woman** whom **Thou gavest** to be with me, **she gave me from the tree** and I ate.' Then the Lord God said to the woman, 'What is this **you** have done?' And the woman said, '**The serpent**

56

deceived me, and I ate.'" (Genesis 3:11-13)

Since the fall of man we have found it difficult to be "naked," or transparent about our faults and wrong actions. If we mess up, like Adam and Eve, we immediately duck into the nearest fig tree with needle and thread in hand, only to emerge with the latest in "fig" fashion. We try to "cover up" any wrong that we have done and then we hastily point the finger of blame at others!

After the Fall, man was unwilling to take responsibility for the failures that occur in relationships.

Getting Even

Finding a way to *get even* with the guilty party usually keeps us preoccupied after an offense has come. We all seem to have our own special way of *getting back* at those who wrong us.

For some, it is flat-out attack. Some are highly skilled at anger, reviling, outbursts, and defending their rights.   These highly explosive folks let you know how they feel — no need to wonder.

Others *get even* in a more civilized manner. They clam up, avoid the perpetrator, and write people off. They are silent, but can be deadly. They often lie in wait for revenge. They might get you to trust them and then, right when you need them the most, abandon you. They can smile at you and then when you are not with them, stab you in the back with their words. These folks keep you guessing.

Then there are those who seem not to care about getting even. Ultimately they do, but it is in a way that is not as obvious as how the others do it. These folks pretend the offense never occurred and just "keep on keeping on." But they never let you get close to them again and the relationship always stays at the same superficial level.

This is pretty typical in an employee/employer relationship. I have heard employees say of their employer, "I just let her rant and rave. I won't be on this job forever — besides the money is good!" The way this person "gets even" is by never giving more to the offender than they are *demanded* to. They are like vitamins; they only produce the "minimum daily requirements."

Still others react to conflict with *divorce* — I'm using the term *divorce* in a broader sense to mean the termination of any existing relationship or union. When you get into a relational wrinkle with these folks, they just split! "Bye bye, Birdie."

A Cry For Justice

No matter how you try to get even with others, one thing is universal. Once we have been wronged, there is a cry for **justice** from within us! To the *natural* man, justice translates into at least making the perpetrator aware of the pain they caused us, if not causing him to experience that *same* pain.

The Old Testament laws of God suited the natural man's tendencies just fine. Leviticus 24:19-20 says, "If a man injures his neighbor, **just as** he has done, **so it shall** be done to him: fracture for fracture, eye for eye, tooth for tooth; **just as** he has injured a man, **so it shall** be inflicted on him."

Can you imagine what it would be like to lose one of your eyes because of an attack from or the negligence of another? Every time you would see the other person, you would think, "I've lost an eye because of *him*! He has two, I only have one. This was *his* fault and he doesn't have to deal with it at all! I have to face people who look at me funny. I have to adjust how I do things because I have lost much of my depth perception. Every time I face someone, I have to deal with embarrassment. He goes on with a little fading guilt and I am bearing the brunt of *his* wrong actions. It isn't fair! He should have his eye plucked out so that he really *knows* the result of his actions. He should experience what he did to me! Then **justice** would be met."

Justice under the Old Testament agreed with this natural approach completely. How one person injured another, "**so it shall** be inflicted on him." Old Covenant justice was eye for eye, tooth for tooth, fracture for fracture. The guilty party was *identified* and *made to suffer* to even the score. The natural man loved this (as long as he wasn't the guilty party!).

But then Jesus came. He shocked everyone.

"You have heard that it was said, 'An eye for an eye, and a tooth for a tooth.' But I say to you, do not resist him who is evil; but whoever slaps you on your right cheek, **turn to him the other also**. And if anyone wants to sue you, and take your shirt, **let him have your coat** also. And whoever shall force you to go one mile, **go with him two**. Give to him who asks of you, and do not turn away from him who wants to borrow from you. You have heard that it was said, 'You shall love your neighbor, and hate your enemy.' But I say to you, **love your enemies**, and pray for those who persecute you in order that you may be sons of your Father who is in heaven; for He causes His sun to rise on the evil and the good, and sends rain on the righteous and the unrighteous. For if you love those who love you, what reward have you? Do not even the tax-gatherers do the same? And if you greet your brothers only, what do you do more than others? Do not even the Gentiles do the same? Therefore you are to be perfect, as your heavenly Father is perfect." (Matthew 5:38-48)

Jesus introduced a radical idea. Now we are to love, not retaliate. Forgive, instead of demanding "payment in full" from those who abuse us. He actually tells us to *be kind* to those who have ripped us off emotionally, socially, or physically! Is He trying to set us up to be abused repeatedly?!?

How can He do that? Who will take the blame and bear the responsibility for wrong actions, if not the person who did the wrong? Where is justice? Where is truth? Something inside us needs to know that the score has been evened before we can begin to forget an incident.

Remember, when conflict comes we have two choices. Either we face it with a *natural human* response or with the *Christian* response. We've just discussed the natural human response, now let's talk about the *Christian* response to conflict.

How God Responds

To understand how the believer is to respond to conflict, we must look at how God responds. How does God act in the midst of conflict?

The Bible says, "All have sinned and fallen short of the glory of God." (Romans 3:23) Because God is just, justice demanded a "pay back" for the wrong we had done. The Bible says, "The wages of sin is **death**." (Romans 6:23) God owed us death.

Justice had to be met. Death was the price that had to be paid.

We were the guilty party and we deserved the payment of death for our sin. But God came up with an amazing "payment plan." He introduced the principle of **substitution**.

On the cross Jesus became **our substitute!** He took the penalty, guilt, and death for *our* sin. "He made Him who knew no sin to be sin **on our behalf**." (2 Corinthians 5:21) God gave the death He owed us to Jesus. Jesus became our substitute by becoming the "guilty party" for our sin. Now, all the relational conflict between God and us is gone, as far as He is concerned!

I once read a true story of a man who ran into a police station crying, "I can't take it anymore, I am the one who murdered that man!" When the officers finally got him to settle down, they discovered that this man had murdered someone 18 years before. After committing the crime, he ran home and hid the bloodied knife in his closet.

His younger brother discovered the blade and, upon hearing of the man's murder, turned himself in to protect his older brother. The older one said nothing as his brother was tried, convicted, and eventually executed for the crime *he* had committed.

As the years went by, guilt ate away at him until he finally broke and came to the police station that day. But there was nothing to be done about it. The crime had already been paid for. The younger brother had become the substitute for the older and the older brother could not be held guilty!

Why did Jesus do what He did for us? Because justice had to be satisfied and He regarded us as too valuable and precious to render to us what we deserved. Instead, He came and took our punishment.

I heard a story of a judge in California who was listening to a case of a young lady who had been given a ticket for speeding. She came into the court room to contest the ticket. After hearing her testimony and the testimony of the officer who issued the ticket, he gave her a verdict of guilty and presented her with a hefty fine.

After he pounded his gavel on the large bench, he stood up, took off his robe and proceeded to the bailiff, with wallet in hand. He paid the fine and told *his daughter* to drive home watching the speed limit this time.

In a very small way, this story captures what God did through the cross. As Judge, He had to pronounce us guilty for the wrong we had done. But as our Creator, He stepped off the throne and came to take the penalty **for us**!

God dealt with the relational conflict caused by man through the principle of *substitution*. As our substitute, Jesus took the blame and the responsibility for **our** wrong actions. Because of the work of the cross, we have been reconciled to God.

Now, every time we offend, attack, or otherwise fail God — He doesn't have to retaliate for justice to be met! Justice has *already been met* in Jesus! In essence, Jesus cried from the cross, "Blame me and release (forgive) them from their sin!"

God allowed Jesus to pay the penalty for all possible wrong we could have done. Jesus bore all our guilt. He was an absolute substitute. Now, there is no barrier between God and us anymore. We can walk together. I Peter 3:18 says, "For Christ died for sins once for all, the righteous for the unrighteous, **to bring you to God**." In Christ, all relational conflict between God and man has been destroyed!

The incredible thing about this is that He forgave us in Christ before there was any evidence that we would respond! He forgave us *before* we asked for forgiveness. He forgave us while we were still actively sinning against Him. Romans 5:8 says, "But God demonstrates His own love for us in this: While we were still sinners, Christ died for us."

Of course we must *receive* this forgiveness to secure a restored relationship with Him, but the point is that before any attempt was made on our part to be restored, He was reaching out to us with forgiveness. "Namely, that God was in Christ reconciling the world to Himself, **not counting their trespasses against them**." (2 Corinthians 5:19)

Our Response to Conflict

Remember what Jesus said in Matthew 5 about "not resisting him who is evil" and "turning the other cheek" and "giving your coat also" and going the "second mile?" Jesus is challenging us to let people do things that we wouldn't normally let them get away with doing. Plus, He is telling us to back off from what would be natural to us: defensiveness and retaliation!

I posed this question before. How could He ask us to do that? What about justice?

The Bible says, "Be kind to one another, tender-hearted, forgiving each other, **just as God in Christ has forgiven you**." This is an amazing command. He is telling us to forgive people who offend **us** *on the same basis* that God forgives us for our offenses.

The basis of God's forgiveness for us is the cross of Calvary. There, God placed upon Jesus both the blame and the punishment for the wrong we had done. He was our **substitute**. God regarded Jesus as the guilty person for justice's sake, and then turned and *released us.*

As wild as it may seem, we are commanded to forgive one another based upon what Jesus did on the cross as well. God does not **suggest** that we forgive those who offend us. **He demands it!** He can because on the cross Jesus saw all the offenses that would come to us and willingly took the blame for them. Now, in our relational conflicts with others, we are to regard Jesus as the guilty person. We must see Him whipped and hanging on a cross for the sins that people have committed against us as well as for those they committed against God. We must allow what Jesus did on the cross to satisfy *our* sense of justice. Then we must turn and release our offenders!

Better let this soak in a moment.

This means that Jesus not only provided for the restoration of man's relationship with God, but for the relationships between men as well!

Just as forgiveness is offered to us based on the cross, we must offer forgiveness to others on that same basis. We must not base our willingness to forgive on what our offenders do. We must not try to "even the score" by making those who offend us *suffer* for their wrongdoing. In our minds, justice should be more than adequately met through Jesus' sacrifice. How could we ever demand more from the offending person than the blood that Jesus offers in their stead?

Think a minute. Remember the Bible says "the wages of sin is death"? God owed us death — eternal separation from Him. Justice demanded we go to hell. Do we believe that Jesus fulfilled the demands for justice?

Yes we do! He was our substitute. He died so we could live. He took on our sin so that we could be forgiven. When God looks at us, He sees our debts "paid in full." Now the Bible says "He is faithful and **just** to forgive us our sins." In other words, God has worked it out so that justice demands we be forgiven instead of sent to hell. Because of Jesus, God would be unjust not to forgive us.

We wronged God. We were destined for hell. Yet, Jesus died *for us* as our substitute so that we could have a relationship with God and go to Heaven. He took our blame. He satisfied justice. In a sense, God "got even" with the world when He poured our sin and His wrath for that sin on Jesus. Jesus took it willingly.

If Jesus' sacrifice was enough to satisfy the demands for justice *within God*, why wouldn't it be enough to satisfy the demands for justice *within us* for the offenses of others toward us? Are we greater than God?

Maybe we feel that the way we have offended God is far less serious than the way others have offended us. Maybe we feel that Jesus' precious blood may be powerful enough to wash away those "minor" offenses we have made toward God but is found wanting when trying to wash away the offenses of others toward us.

Does Jesus' sacrifice mean so little to us that it does not satisfy our personal cry for justice — our need to "get even?" Isn't it a slap in the Master's face to demand more than God Himself has demanded? Are you sure you must make the person who offended you suffer before you are satisfied? Jesus is crying out, "Blame me and let them go!"

Once the Apostle Peter asked Jesus some questions about forgiving those who offend us. Jesus gave him a parable about a

65

king who forgave a man over six billion dollars of debt. In the parable the king represents God; the man, each of us. The man (us) whom the king (God) forgave turned and refused to forgive someone who owed him two thousand dollars —— virtually nothing in comparison to what the man owed and was forgiven of by the king. The one who owed the two thousand begged and pleaded to be given more time to repay, but his "forgiven" creditor refused to wait and had him thrown into jail. Let's pick up the narrative and see the king's response in Matthew 18:31-35.

"Then the man's friends went to the king and told him what had happened. And the king called before him the man he had forgiven and said, 'You evil hearted wretch! Here I forgave you all that tremendous debt, just because you asked me to —— shouldn't you have mercy on others, just as I had mercy on you?'

Can you imagine actually being forgiven of billions of dollars only to turn and refuse to forgive what in comparison would be pennies? That is what we do when we think lightly of God forgiving us and yet refuse to forgive people who offend us. Look at what the king said in response to this:

"Then the angry king sent the man to the torture chamber until he had paid every penny due. **So shall my heavenly Father do to you if you refuse to truly forgive your brothers.**"

Now, instead of reacting *naturally* to conflict, and "getting even" with people in our own way, we must respond like God.

Remember God's "payment plan?" The principle of **substitution?** We must allow Jesus to become the *substitute* for **our** offender.

On the cross Jesus did more than open the way for us to have relational resolve with God. **He opened the door for us to resolve our conflicts with one another in a new way** — in a way that is not dependent upon the one who is causing the conflict.

As believers, we must see Jesus becoming the guilty party on the tree and bearing the guilt of all sin committed **against us**. Then we must choose to release (forgive) the person that offended us. This is how the Christian deals with conflict.

There is something inside us that cringes about this. We want to "get even" with the person who has wronged us! But we must stop majoring in anger, reviling, outbursts, defending our rights, clamming up, writing people off, etc. We must let go of that part of us that does not want to accept what Jesus has done and wants to "get back" at the person who offended us. We must die to those feelings — crucify them.

This miracle of substitution (Jesus taking the blame for the person who is guilty) opens the way for us to be reconciled to each other. We no longer have to count the trespasser's actions against him! Now every time others offend, attack, or otherwise fail us — we don't have to retaliate for justice to be met. We don't have to try to "get even" or "crucify" them. We must hear Jesus crying from the cross, "Blame me and release (forgive) them from their sin!" This is the miracle of the cross!

Our Onesimus

When the Apostle Paul contacts Philemon in the book of the same name, he refers to a slave of Philemon, named Onesimus. Evidently the slave, Onesimus, had run away from Philemon and had stolen some things from him. Paul had met Onesimus while he was in prison and won him to Christ.

Onesimus wanted to make things right between himself and Philemon, whom Paul also knew. Paul writes to Philemon asking him to forgive Onesimus. "I appeal to you for my child, whom I have begotten in my imprisonment, Onesimus, whom I wished to keep with me, that in your behalf he might minister to me in my imprisonment for the gospel; but without your consent I did not want to do anything, that your goodness should not be as it were by compulsion, but of your own free will." (Philemon 10, 13-14)

Onesimus was probably an unclosed chapter in Philemon's life. Paul shows that Philemon thought Onesimus was "useless" (V. 11). Apparently Philemon had been mistreated through what the slave had done. Now Paul asks him to allow Onesimus to "represent" Philemon in serving Paul (V. 13).

I would imagine that this was a tough thing for Philemon to do. What about justice? He had been robbed by this slave as well as left "short handed" as far as workers were concerned.

Philemon would have to forgive Onesimus of his past debts before he could believe there was a new man inside that old "useless" thief. He would have to get a new perspective of Onesimus before agreeing to let the slave "represent" him. The apostle was an important man! He probably thought, "Let me send you someone who is faithful and throw that guy to the gallows!"

Paul goes on to ask Philemon to view Onesimus in a new way,

"**[View him]** no longer as a slave, but more than a slave, a beloved brother, especially to me, but how much more to you, both in flesh and in the Lord. **If then you regard me** a partner, accept him **as you would me**. But if he has wronged you in any way, or owes you anything, **charge that to my account**; I, Paul, am writing this with my own hand, I will repay it (lest I should mention to you that you owe to me even your own self as well)." (Philemon 16-19)

He asks Philemon, who thinks very highly of the Apostle Paul, to view Onesimus no longer as a slave, but as an equal with the Apostle, and with himself. In case Philemon couldn't get past some things that Onesimus has done, Paul says, "If he has wronged you in any way, or owes you anything, **charge that to my account**."

I don't think you can get a clearer picture of what Jesus is asking us to do when it comes to the Onesimuses of our lives — to those who have indebted themselves to us for whatever reason.

In essence, Jesus is saying, "I appeal to you for my child, whom I have begotten in my imprisonment (whom I have died for), your Onesimus (your spouse, child, relative, authority figure, organization, etc.).

"But without your consent I did not want to do anything, that your goodness should not be as it were by compulsion, but of your own free will (choose to forgive him!). No longer view your Onesimus as a slave (as indebted to you), but more than a slave, as a beloved brother (for I died for him).

"If then you regard Me as a partner, accept him as you would Me. But if he has wronged you in any way, or owes you anything, charge that to my account (I bore the debt on Calvary). I, Jesus, am telling you this; I will repay it (lest I should mention to you that you owe to me even your own self as well)."

When the Christian church realizes that they are the tangible, living, pulsating body—flesh and bones and blood and brain of Jesus Christ—and that God is manifesting through each one every minute, and is endeavoring to accomplish His will for the world through them, then Christian service and responsibility will be understood.

John G. Lake

6

WE ARE HIS REPRESENTATIVES

As believers in Jesus Christ, we are not to represent *ourselves* in our attitudes and actions upon this earth. We are the "Body of Christ!" Paul said, "Or do you not recognize this about yourselves, that Jesus Christ is in you?" (2 Corinthians 13:5)

When Jesus walked the earth, He used to say, "He who has seen me has seen the Father." (John 14:9) We should be able to say, "He who has seen me has seen Jesus!" 1 John 4:17 says, "As He (Jesus) is, so also are **we** in this world."

We are Christ's people, His representatives, His ambassadors! We are to portray His likeness. As the moon reflects the borrowed light of the *sun*, we are to reflect the borrowed eternal light of the *Son* of God!

In relationships we are to reflect *God's* attitudes and heart, not our natural human ones. In Titus 3:2-6, Paul lays out the difference between how we *used to* face our relationships with others and how we are to face them today.

"Malign no one, be uncontentious, gentle, showing every consideration for all men. For **we also once were** foolish ourselves, disobedient, deceived, enslaved to various lusts and pleasures, spending our life in **malice** and **envy, hateful**, and **hating one another**. But when the **kindness** of God our Savior and **His love for mankind appeared**, He saved us."

As unbelievers we used to respond to conflict by maligning others, being full of contention, showing no consideration. We were filled with malice and envy, we were hateful and hated people. That is the "way of the world!" We could only respond to others based upon *the way* they treated us. If they were kind to us, we were kind to them. If they hated us, we hated them. Our response to people was dependent upon *how they acted.*

Here Paul says we are no longer to respond to people based upon how they act toward us! He says we all have made mistakes. We have all been foolish, deceived and enslaved to stupid actions that affected others around us. Then he points out how God responded to our wrong actions. He says that God had a love for man and a kindness toward us that was not based upon what we have done. He shows that God, based upon a **mercy** that was in Him, chose to reach out to us and pour upon us a **grace** that cleansed and changed us. He washed away all the failures and conflicts of our past and positioned us with a bright new future in

Him!

Paul challenges us to treat others in a new way based upon how God has chosen to treat us! As portraits of Christ we are to respond to and treat others *the way* He treats us! That is what Jesus meant when He said,

"But I say to you, love your enemies, and pray for those who persecute you **in order that you may be sons of your Father** who is in heaven; for He causes His sun to rise on the evil and the good, and sends rain on the righteous and the unrighteous. For if you love those who love you, what reward have you? Do not even the tax-gatherers do the same? And if you greet your brothers only, what do you do more than others? Do not even the Gentiles do the same? Therefore **you are to be perfect, as your heavenly Father** is perfect." (Matthew 5:44-48)

The unbeliever doesn't necessarily see and understand God when we believe and preach right doctrine. They usually think we are just being "religious." Typically, the unbeliever doesn't discern or comprehend God through our praise and worship services or through our commitment to morality and high ethical standards. They just think we are weird or old fashioned! They think Catholics have mass, Buddhists burn incense, Mormons wear funny underclothes, and "born-againers" brag about being holier than everyone else.

But the unbeliever can relate to kindness and nonjudgmentalism. When they see these traits in the believer consistently, they know it is not native human behavior and they will ask about it. "Why are you like this?", they'll ask. When you tell them it isn't just you, but God's attitude toward them reaching out through you, they will clearly *see* and *understand* God.

Paul said in another place, "We are ambassadors for Christ, as though God were entreating through us." (2 Corinthians 5:20) That is the believer! We are to represent God in all our relational dealings.

This may shock you, but God measures our love for Him by *how we treat* our fellow man. 1 John 4:20 says, "If someone says, 'I love God,' and hates his brother, he is a liar; for the one who **does not love his brother** whom he has seen, **cannot love God** whom he has not seen."

Jesus, referring to a day in the future, said,

"Then the King will say to those on His right, 'Come, you who are blessed of My Father, inherit the kingdom prepared for you from the foundation of the world. For I was hungry, and you gave Me something to eat; I was thirsty, and you gave Me drink; I was a stranger, and you invited Me in; naked, and you clothed Me; I was sick, and you visited Me; I was in prison, and you came to Me.' Then the righteous will answer Him, saying, 'Lord, when did we see You hungry, and feed You, or thirsty, and give You drink? And when did we see You a stranger, and invite You in, or naked, and clothe You? And when did we see You sick, or in prison, and come to You?' And the King will answer and say to them, 'Truly I say to you, to the extent that you did it to **one of these** brothers of Mine, even the least of them, **you did it to Me**.'" (Matthew 25:34-40)

Next, let's look at *who* should take the responsibility for moving a relationship toward resolve once conflict appears.

If possible, so far as it depends on you,
    be at peace with all men.

Ro 12:18 NAS

7

TAKING RESPONSIBILITY

I was on my way home from work, longing to throw my body on the couch and just "crash out." All day at the office, it seemed like everyone had been pecking like woodpeckers at my brain, needing something from me. So by the time I started home, I was weary and looking forward to resting in my citadel of peace.

I had no idea that Gail was looking forward to me coming home as well. She had been struggling all day with our jelly-faced toddlers and had put off some important projects until I came home to "help."

I was looking for "rest"; she was looking for "help." We were headed for disaster!

I walked in and grunted "Hi."

She immediately said, "Hi Honey, will you move the couch for me and then watch the baby while I . . .?" She paused because she was reading the negative body language I was throwing at her. She grumbled, "Never mind, I'll do it *all* myself!"

Immediately my defense mechanisms mounted and I trumpeted, "I have had a rough day."

"And I haven't?" she retorted . . . and we were off to the races.

Now, who do you think is responsible for dealing with the tension here? (Now be nice. Remember, I'm the "expert" writing this book.) If you say I was, as the husband, you are wrong. If you say Gail was, as the wife, you are wrong. Who is responsible then? *The one who first realizes that tension has infiltrated the situation.* Let me explain.

Biblically, the responsibility to heal broken relationships does not belong to the one who has wrinkled the relationship. The *responsibility* is determined by who is *aware* of the conflict.

If you are *aware* that a conflict exists between you and another human being, whether the conflict was caused by your actions or not, *you* are responsible to move the relationship toward wholeness.

"If therefore you are presenting your offering at the altar, and there **remember** that your brother has something against you, **leave** your offering there before the altar, and **go** your way; first be reconciled to your brother, and then come and present your offering." (Matthew 5:23-24)

Jesus is telling us that if we *are aware* **we have offended** our brother or sister, we must *go to them* and start the **process** of reconciliation (sometimes it takes time!). In other words, *we are* responsible for the relationship once we are *aware* of the dysfunction.

On the other hand, "If a brother **sins against you**, go to him privately and confront him with his fault." (Matthew 18:15, TLB). Here Jesus tells us if we *are aware* **someone has sinned against us** (we are not even the guilty party here), we are still responsible to *go to them* and confront the situation! Again, *we are* responsible for relational resolve once we are *aware* that there is a wrinkle —— **no matter who is at fault!**

Just as a farmer can predict the future of his field by the seed that he sows, your actions are the "seeds" that can predict the future of every relationship you have. **WITH GOD, YOU CAN TAKE RESPONSIBILITY!**

The enemy will tell you your problem is other people: if only your spouse didn't pick so much, if they were only a little more spiritual, if they just gave you more space, if their personality wasn't like it is, etc. Satan will give you every excuse in the book on why your relationship is the way it is, but it will always be the *other guy's fault.* He will say, "You could get along with *that guy* at work, but he's so difficult." You could really have a great relationship with your boss, but *he* never shows interest in you. You could make this ministry thrive, but those *other workers* are so uncommitted!"

When Jesus came, He brought this radical idea —— "Do not resist him who is evil; but whoever slaps you on your right cheek, **turn to him the other also**. And if anyone wants to sue you, and take your shirt, **let him have your coat** also. And whoever shall force you to go one mile, **go with him two**. Give to him who asks of you, and do not turn away from him who wants to borrow from you. You have heard that it was said, 'You shall love your neighbor, and hate your enemy.' But I say to you, **love your enemies**, and pray for those who persecute you."

Jesus challenges us to go "the second mile" when we have been misused. It is the "second mile" action that releases God's power to bring change in the lives of those with whom we relate. The Scriptures teach us, "If possible, so far as it depends on you, be at peace with all men." (Romans 12:18)

Now, instead of focussing on getting revenge when we are wronged or writing people off when they offend us, **we must** sow actions and attitudes toward them that will lead toward resolving the relationship! Even if a relationship has taken on "enemy status," we still have at our disposal supernatural seed that will cause the relationship to eventually be restored. "But if your enemy is hungry, feed him, and if he is thirsty, give him drink; for in so doing you will heap burning coals upon his head. Do not be overcome by evil, **but overcome evil with good**." (Romans 12:20-21)

God Takes Responsibility

In our relationship with God, *who* is the one responsible for conflict? Isn't it *always* man who offends God? Though *we are the guilty party*, **who takes responsibility** for restoring us? It is always God.

We didn't seek God in order to be saved. "There is none righteous, not even one; there is none who understands, there is none who seeks for God." (Romans 3:10-11) He sought us out and attracted us to Himself. "No one can come unto Me, **unless**

80

the Father who sent Me draws him; every one who has heard and learned **from the Father** comes to Me." (John 6:44-45) We didn't love God for Him to love us. "We love Him, because He **first** loved us." (1 John 4:19)

The point is, Christianity has never been our responsibility. It is our response to *His* ability!

We have always assumed that the "guilty party" is the one who is *responsible* for restoring broken relationships. But that is not true in God's relationship with man. Remember that how He deals with relational conflict is our example of how we are to act and take responsibility in our dealings with others:

"And be kind to one another, tender-hearted, forgiving each other, **just as God** in Christ also has forgiven you. Therefore **be imitators of God**, as beloved children; and walk in love, **just as Christ** also loved you, and gave Himself up for us, an offering and a sacrifice to God as a fragrant aroma." (Ephesians 4:32-5:2)

"The one who says he abides in Him ought himself to walk in the same manner as **He walked**." (1 John 2:6)

"In this is love, not that we loved God, but that He loved us and sent His Son to be the propitiation for our sins. Beloved, if God so loved us, **we also ought to love one another**." (1 John 4:10-11)

Again, the responsibility to heal broken relationships is not to be left to the one who wrinkled the relationship, but *responsibility belongs to the one who is aware of the conflict.* If you are *aware* that a conflict exists between you and another human being, whether you caused the conflict or not, *you* are responsible to see that the conflict resolves.

Friend, your relationships don't have to fail and die because of the wrong actions of others. There is a supernatural provision called *forgiveness* that was purchased as Jesus was beaten upon His back and forced to go through the physical horror of the cross.

He cried out through that experience, "Father forgive them, they know not what they are doing." This great statement is the power of forgiveness in action that will enable all relationships to move toward wholeness.

All of us have failed. Forgiveness is looking past a person's failure and expecting them to change. Somehow, God uses this perspective of faith in others with our continued "second mile" acts of love and kindness to transform an evil person.

The great martyr Stephen knew of the power of facing his relationships this way. In Acts 7, he was preaching his heart out to the Jews who in turn "began gnashing their teeth at him."

They finally "cried out with a loud voice, and covered their ears, and rushed upon him with one impulse" and began stoning him to death.

Stephen was just trying to help them. When they responded this way he could have picked up the stones and started throwing them back! But he knew the forgiving heart of Jesus. Stephen prayed as he was being stoned, "'Lord Jesus, receive my spirit!' And falling on his knees, he cried out with a loud voice, 'Lord, do not hold this sin against them!' And having said this, he fell asleep." (Acts 7:59-60)

Overcoming the Evil in Others

The wonderful thing about all this is that when we choose to release people who are guilty, it opens the door for God to move in their lives. "But if your enemy is hungry, feed him, and if he is thirsty, give him drink; for in so doing you will heap burning coals upon his head. Do not be overcome by evil, but overcome evil with good." (Romans 12:20-21)

How did God overcome the evil that was present in Stephen's case? In verse 58 of chapter 7 we read, "And when they had driven him out of the city, they began stoning him, and the witnesses laid aside their robes at the feet of a young man named Saul."

Saul was the instigator of this event. In fact, he was working overtime to destroy the Church of Jesus Christ. He was the channel for the "evil" that killed Stephen. But through Stephen's willingness to be a vessel of forgiveness, even when it meant his death; he opened the door for God to overcome the "evil" that was present in Saul.

"Now Saul, still breathing threats and murder against the disciples of the Lord, went to the high priest, and asked for letters from him to the synagogues at Damascus, so that if he found any belonging to the Way, both men and women, he might bring them bound to Jerusalem.

"And it came about that as he journeyed, he was approaching Damascus, and suddenly a light from heaven flashed around him; and he fell to the ground, and heard a voice saying to him, 'Saul, Saul, why are you persecuting Me?' And he said, 'Who art thou, Lord?' And He said, 'I am Jesus whom you are persecuting." (Acts 9:1-5)

Later Saul said, "I was not disobedient to the heavenly vision . . ." (Acts 26:19)

This man Saul had created havoc for the whole church. After his salvation the Scripture says, "So the church throughout all Judea and Galilee and Samaria enjoyed peace." (Acts 9:31) If confronting Saul in such a dramatic way was just a sovereign act of God, not initiated by man, why doesn't God just do it to everyone and then take us to heaven?

It was more than sovereignty that paved the way for this conversion. It was *Stephen's* act of forgiveness that opened the door for God to blast through and stop this evil man! It was his refusal to avenge the wrong done to him personally. It was his willingness to release the whole matter to God. He wasn't just chattering when he cried, "Lord, do not hold this sin against them!" He meant that from his heart. He had allowed God to influence him to genuinely love those people, looking past their faults and recognizing they were the ones for whom Christ died.

This "feeding of his enemy," this "giving of drink," opened the door for God to pour "burning coals" upon Saul's head and "overcome the evil with good."

In Isaiah 6, Isaiah the prophet had a vision of God and an encounter with some coals. In the vision he cried out, "'Woe to me!' I cried. 'I am ruined! For I am a man of unclean lips, and I live among a people of unclean lips, and my eyes have seen the King, the LORD Almighty.'"

Watch how God responds to Isaiah's uncleanness: "Then one of the seraphs flew to me with a **live coal** in his hand, which he had taken with tongs from the altar. With it he touched my mouth and said, 'See, this has touched your lips; **your guilt is taken away and your sin atoned for**.'"

Biblically, fire symbolizes the purging away of evil. Naturally speaking, we know fire is a purifying, cleansing agent. We use fire to purify metals. It is used to sterilize things. Numbers 31:23 says, "And anything else that can withstand fire must be put through the fire, and **then it will be clean**."

When God speaks of cleansing His people from the effects of evil, He talks of fire. In Jeremiah 23:29, God says, "'Is not my word **like fire**,' declares the LORD."

Paul is telling us that by loving our enemies it gives God the right to put *coals of fire upon their heads*. The result is that He can purge away the forces of evil that are *making them* your enemy and actually **change them**!

Saul was later called Paul the Apostle, and is the one who was responsible for writing a third of the New Testament, instead of destroying the Church — all because someone discovered the power behind the cross, the power of forgiveness.

You and I may never need to sow our lives in martyrdom to see God's power to change others, but we are all called to forgive our spouses, children, employees or employer, fellow church members, etc. when they offend us. We must quit writing people off because they are hard to deal with and start trusting God to move in our relationships to bring unity. We must choose to take *personal responsibility* for the relational conflict we have.

If we do nothing, God will do nothing. Satan knows that. He knows each believer has the enablement of God to mend broken relationships. He is also aware of the resulting power that flows when unity is present. Hence, his strategy is to get you to do nothing and to blame the other guy. "You're justified in not dealing with that person any longer," he'll say. "Write them off!"

Remember, his scheme is to get you and me to think that the people we know cause our struggles.   He wants you and me in *disunity* because he knows that will grieve the Holy Spirit and cripple our prayer life.

Remember our simple rule: *Tension demands attention.*   "If possible, so far as it depends on you, be at peace with all men." (Romans 12:18) "So then let us **pursue** the things which make for peace and the building up of one another." (Romans 14:19)

If you are going to bring resolve into any conflict you must use the power of forgiveness.

Since nothing we intended is ever faultless, and nothing we attempt ever without error, and nothing we achieve without some measure of finitude and fallibility we call humanness, we are saved by forgiveness.

David Augsburger

8

HOW TO FORGIVE PEOPLE

How do you go about forgiving someone who has offended you or wounded you emotionally? Someone might have said something or done something that has caused you to draw back from them. You're in a state of *un*-giving — you can't give them a smile, a conversation, your trust, your kindness, etc.

That is precisely what unforgiveness is -- the state of UN-giving. Forgiveness is *"for"-"giving."* When you're in UN-forgiveness you are in a state of not being able to give.

When Jesus taught on prayer He said,

"Therefore I say to you, all things for which you pray and ask, believe that you have received them, and they shall be

granted you. And whenever you stand praying, forgive, if
you have anything against anyone; so that your Father also
who is in heaven may forgive you your transgressions. But
if **you do not** forgive, **neither will your Father** who is in
heaven forgive your transgressions." (Mark 11:24-26)

Jesus is telling us that if we are going into prayer to ask God to
move in our lives, we must not be in a posture of unforgiveness.
If we are, God can't give us anything because we have locked up
the flow of blessing. Let me explain.
The blessings of God are meant to flow from God to us, and
then from us to others.

"Blessed be the God and Father of our Lord Jesus Christ, the
Father of mercies and God of all comfort; Who comforts us
in all our affliction **so that we may be able to comfort
those** who are in any affliction **with the comfort with
which we ourselves are comforted by God**." (2
Corinthians 1:3-4)

Here, Paul says the comfort he received from God was used to
comfort others. When we choose to withhold from others what
God has blessed us with, we *restrict* the divine flow — we are in
unforgiveness or "un-giving." God can no longer continue to give
to us as freely as He desires. Jesus said, "Freely you have
received, **freely give**."
Let's look at four steps you can take to forgive or release
people when they offend you.

Step 1
Understand the "Why?" behind the incident.
If you can identify *why* an event has happened, it will aid in the forgiveness process. *Understanding* always makes the process simpler. Dr. Charles Stanley, in his book entitled *Forgiveness*, tells a story that shows how understanding helps to improve our attitudes toward people.

"Once there was a boy who lived with his mother and grandfather. His grandfather was not really an elderly man, but he was confined to a wheelchair and had very little use of his arms. His face was badly scarred, and he had a difficult time swallowing his food.

"Every day the little boy was assigned the task of going into his grandfather's room and feeding him lunch. This the little boy did faithfully, but not joyously. It was quite a mess to feed Grandfather.

"As the boy grew into adolescence, he became weary of his responsibility. One day he stormed into the kitchen and announced that he had had enough. He told his mother, 'From now on, you can feed Grandfather.'

"Very patiently his mother turned from her chores, motioned for her son to sit down, and said, 'You are a young man now. It is time you knew the whole truth about your grandfather.' She continued, 'Grandfather has not always been confined to a wheelchair. In fact he used to be quite an athlete. When you were a baby, however, there was an accident.'

"The boy leaned forward in his chair as his mother began to cry.

"She said, 'There was a fire. Your father was working in the basement, and he thought you were upstairs with me. I thought

89

he was downstairs with you. We both rushed out of the house leaving you alone upstairs. Your grandfather was visiting at the time. He was the first to realize what happened. Without a word he went back into the house, found you, wrapped you in a wet blanket, and made a mad dash through the flames. He brought you safely to your father and me.

"'He was rushed to the emergency room suffering from second- and third-degree burns as well as smoke inhalation. The reason he is the way he is today is because of what he suffered the day he saved your life.'

"By this time the boy had tears in his eyes as well. He never knew; his grandfather never told him. And with no conscious effort on his part, his attitude changed. With no further complaints, he picked up his grandfather's lunch tray and took it to his room."[1]

It often helps the forgiveness process when you understand why people act the way they do.

Have you ever misjudged someone? It is easy to do! We tend to judge others by their **actions** and to judge ourselves by our **intentions** —— so we tend to be much more tolerant of ourselves. We intended to mow the lawn, so, in a way, we did. "Why is my wife so angry with me . . . **she** needs to get her attitude under control." (We're quick to pass the buck!)

She thinks, "He didn't mow it —— he doesn't care about this family! He *never* does anything around here, but if one of his 'buddies' calls for help or counsel, he has all the time in the world!"

Instead of always jumping to conclusions, learn to pause in order to *understand* what is really going on. Ask the Holy Spirit to help you when you sense tension mounting!

This is how Jesus operated.

"And He (Jesus) will delight in the fear of the Lord, and He will not judge by what His eyes see, nor make a decision by what His ears hear." (Isaiah 11:3)

Many factors like personality, background, stress, maturity levels (spiritually, emotionally), direct satanic attack, etc., affect the way people act. Pausing to try to understand will really help you in the forgiving process.

When John and Sarah walked into my office, I was surprised to learn their marriage was close to breaking up. John and Sarah seemed to be a wonderful couple. They were both the kind of people you would be honored to have as friends. Yet, as wonderful as they were, they still had problems in their marriage. A lot of it had to do with background.

John grew up in a home where both his parents were quiet, and seldom, if ever, raised their voices. In John's home, raising your voice meant you were extremely angry. Sarah, on the other hand, grew up in a larger family where you had to yell or you lost your opportunity to get the potatoes at the other end of the dinner table. The only time her family got quiet was when they were stewing in anger.

When incidents that needed discussion arose after Sarah and John married, Sarah would naturally begin to raise her voice. John would think, "Oh my, I'd better not say another word. She has lost her temper!"

As John walked silently out of the room thinking he was helping the situation, Sarah would think, "Why won't he talk to me? Why

91

is he so angry?"

They totally misunderstood each other.

Satan loves to take these times of misunderstanding and twist us up inside so that we feel victimized! We know from Luke 4:13 that he is always looking for an "opportune time".

Satan Instigates Wrong Action

Once, when Jesus was sharing with His disciples, Peter took Him aside and began to try to pressure Him into a wrong decision. Instead of getting angry with Peter, Jesus perceived that His disciple had listened to a wrong voice. Jesus responded, **"Get behind Me, Satan! You are a stumbling block to Me**; for you are not setting your mind on God's interests, but man's.'" (Matthew 16:21-23)

Jesus recognized that Peter was not to blame for what he was saying, though he should have been more cautious with his mouth!

Realize there are times when people will act as a result of the influence of Satan. I am not saying they are demon possessed; I am saying they get influenced to say and do things that they wouldn't have said or done by themselves. In Ephesians 2:1-3 we read,

> "And you were dead in your trespasses and sins, in which you formerly walked **according to** the course of this world, **according to** the prince of the power of the air, of the spirit that is **now working in** the sons of disobedience. Among them we too all formerly lived in the lusts of our flesh, indulging the desires of the flesh and of the mind, and were by nature children of wrath, even as the rest."

Apart from Jesus Christ, much of how we think and act is "according to" forces beyond ourselves — forces of darkness. This is the "why?" behind many of the heinous offenses that occur in the earth where innocent people are victimized.

There are evil spirits who specialize in driving people to murder, rape, incest, thievery, physical or emotional abuse, etc. Remember the words of Paul in Ephesians 6:10, "For our struggle is not against **flesh and blood**, but against the rulers, against the powers, against the world forces of this darkness, against the spiritual forces of wickedness in the heavenly places."

According to Ephesians 4:27, Christians can be influenced by evil spirits if we are not watchful. "And do not give place to the devil." (KJV) But not every wrong action producing conflict is caused by a *direct* working of Satan. He always gets involved at some point, but many conflicts are caused by people being selfish or touchy. The Bible calls it being "carnal."

Other Contributing Factors
The Corinthian Church had a lot of relational trouble. Paul said the reason for it was that the Corinthians were "carnal." In other words, they were letting their fallen human natures govern how they responded to each other.

"And I, brethren, could not speak to you as to spiritual men, but as to men of flesh, as to babes in Christ . . . for you are still fleshly. Since there is **jealousy and strife among you**, are you not fleshly, and are you not walking like mere men?" (1 Corinthians 3:1-3)

93

Sometimes people will act wrong, not because of a direct working of hell, but because they have misread the action or statement of another. Then they let their natural sinful nature dominate them and may angrily lash out against innocent bystanders.

Other times people come across offensively. Reacting to pain from the hurts that they have experienced, they are really trying to protect themselves from being injured again. Wounded animals do not act predictably when you approach them; neither do emotionally wounded humans.

No matter what reason causes the offense, Satan eventually gets involved, either to **instigate** the offense or to **agitate** it once it comes. His true motive is to get you to fester in unforgiveness. That, to him, is monumentally more important than the incident that hurt you to begin with! Do not give him that chance.

Remember that Satan can take advantage of us when we are in unforgiveness! "But whom you forgive anything, I forgive also; for indeed what I have forgiven, if I have forgiven anything, I did it for your sakes in the presence of Christ, in order that **no advantage be taken of us by Satan**; for we are not ignorant of his schemes." (2 Corinthians 2:10-11)

Again, no matter what causes the offense, Satan gets involved, either to instigate it or to agitate it once it comes. We must choose to take authority over **his** involvement first, whenever tension appears in our relationships with others.

When God dealt with Adam and Eve in the fall, He got to the root of the problem first — Satan. *Then* He dealt with Adam and Eve:

"And the Lord God said to the serpent, 'Because you have

done this, cursed are you . . .' (Genesis 3:14)

"To the woman He said, . . . (V. 16)

"Then to Adam He said . . ." (V. 17)

When tension arises, keep this perspective. It is important to deal with the people who have been involved in the conflict, but decide to deal with the root of the problem first — Satan. The Bible says we can "cast out devils" (Mark 16:17). When relational tension comes, command Satan to leave! Then deal with the people involved.

Even if you cannot determine the *"why?"* behind the incident — continue the process of forgiveness anyway. Knowing why an incident occurs only *helps* us forgive, it is not *essential* to the process!

Step 2

Separate the person from their sin.

To do this you must keep in mind the miracle of the cross!

"Namely, that God was in Christ reconciling the world to Himself, **not counting their trespasses against them**, and He has committed to us the word of reconciliation." (2 Corinthians 5:19)

The Greek word translated forgiveness, *aphieemi*, is used 146 times in the Greek New Testament. Of the 146 times it is used, it is only translated "forgiveness" 49 times. It is translated other times as, "left," "sent away," "shall be left," "forsook," etc.

In Gerhard Kittel's *Theological Dictionary of the New Testament*, Dr. Kittle says *aphieemi* means "to send off, to release, to let go or to let be." But my favorite definition is when he says the word could be translated, "to hurl (e.g., missiles)". When you apply the blood of Jesus to a sin you have committed, it causes that sin to be hurled from you like a missile blasting away! It leaves forever![2]

What a picture that paints for us! When God forgives us, He "sends away" our sins. There is no evidence that they were ever with us!

"As far as the east is from the west, so far has He removed our transgressions from us." (Psalm 103:12)

"For thou hast cast all my sins behind Thy back." (Isaiah 38:17)

"He will again have compassion on us; He will tread our iniquities underfoot. Yes, Thou wilt cast all our sins into the depths of the sea." (Micah 7:19)

This is the way we are to forgive each other! "...Forgiving each other, **just as God** in Christ has forgiven you." (Ephesians 4:32) When we forgive others, we must "send away" their sins. There should be no evidence of their transgression lingering in our minds!

Now, when you look at the person you have forgiven, refuse to focus on the offense. Center on the fact that this is one for whom Christ has died. God says they are worth Jesus! Learning to separate men from their sin opens the door for you to help bring them out of it.

Get the Log Out

"Do not judge lest you be judged. For in the way you judge, you will be judged; and by your standard of measure, it will be measured to you. And why do you look at the **speck** that is in your brother's eye, but do not notice the **log** that is in your own eye? Or how can you say to your brother, 'Let me take the **speck** out of your eye', and behold, the **log** is in your own eye? You hypocrite, **first take the log out** of your own eye, and then **you will see clearly** to take the **speck** out of your brother's eye." (Matthew 7:1-5)

While my wife Gail and I were attending Bible school, we met one of the nicest people we have ever met. Bill was a caring and trusted friend. The only real problem we had with him was that he did not carry his own weight financially. He would continually ask us for rides home, borrow our car, use our phone, eat our meals, come over to our apartment on hot summer days to keep from having to turn on his air conditioner, etc.

At first it did not bother me. I grew up in a home where we always shared what we had with others. But over time it began to bother me that Bill never even offered to chip in with expenses he was helping to incur.

By our second year of school, the situation was getting old. It eventually got so bad that I could no longer look at Bill without thinking about how he was using us. I knew I couldn't talk with him while I was upset because it would really hurt him. And, even though it was wrong, I began acting on my feelings by avoiding him at school and leaving the room when he visited our apartment.

At one point I commented to Gail, "He is getting on my nerves so much, I feel like punching him!" She told me I had better deal with my feelings before I said something I would regret — so I finally made it a matter of prayer.

A few days later, as I was exiting a freeway ramp, God spoke to me. He said, "You're making his splinter a log."

"What?", I asked.

"You're making his splinter a log," He repeated.

I was driving with my eyes wide open and at the same time clearly viewing a mini-movie inside myself. I saw our friend Bill, who had become "the cheapskate" in my mind, with what looked like a little thorn sticking out of his eye. As I lifted my hand to the thorn, an exact duplicate appeared between my thumb and index finger. In the inner vision I saw myself taking the duplicate splinter and bringing it so close to my face that all I saw was the splinter — *it had gotten so large it became a log!*

The Lord was trying to show me that I had lost sight of the fact that Bill was a precious brother **with** a problem (or splinter). Instead, in my eyes, he actually *became* the problem (a log).

The Lord reminded me of the verse in Matthew 7 and said I could help Bill *if* I would "first take the log" out of my own eye, and then I would "see clearly to take the speck" out of my brother's eye.

The next day when I saw Bill, I saw him with a new set of eyes. He was now a precious brother with a problem instead of a problem brother. That is when I knew I could speak with him without judgment and without hurting him. I approached him, but before I could say a word he said, "Ed, God began dealing with me yesterday about taking advantage of you and Gail. I need to be more responsible . . . please take this $20 as a start . . . I'm really sorry."

To forgive Bill, I had to separate him from his sin. This separation opened the door for change to come —— **in both of us!** Forgiving and releasing people from their sins is God's way of bringing restoration. It also sets the stage for necessary change in people. By not forgiving people, we hinder God from touching them through us.

Step 3
Make the decision.
Make the decision to release the person who has offended you. Forgiveness is not a feeling; it is an act of your will —— a **quality decision**.

A quality decision is a decision from which there is no retreat! You have decided to release the person from his guilt. You may remember the offense repeatedly at first. That is o.k. The commitment to forgive a person is a commitment to "send away" the incident every time it *reappears* in your mind!

Once the Apostle Peter asked Jesus, "'Lord, how often shall my brother sin against me and I forgive him? Up to seven times?' Jesus said to him, 'I do not only say to you, up to seven times, but up to seventy times seven.'" (Matthew 18:21-22) That makes four hundred and ninety times.

Then Luke, in his gospel, adds the phrase, "in one day." Imagine forgiving the same person 490 times a day! I call it the *490 Principle*.

Listen to how author Cash Godbold applied this principle: "I had a terrible problem with a person in life. I felt he had let me down when I was in desperate need and that thing totally consumed me. I'd think about it five, ten times a day and all the anger and bitterness of my soul came out against that person. Then I found this principle of forgiveness and it got to where it was only three or four times a day it would come up. And every time it came up I thought — four hundred ninety times — and I would forgive. After a few months it came up only a couple times a week and then maybe once a month. Today, I can't even remember the last time I thought about it. It's marvelous; it's liberating to get rid of that garbage in my life. Guess what? That person hasn't asked to be forgiven, but I'm free of the garbage."[3]

The choice to forgive means to keep doing it every time the memory of the incident arises. At first that might be many times a day. Each time, release it to God. After a short time, you will find the incident losing strength and you will find new victory in God. Keep in mind this is the same way you must forgive yourself!

Step 4
Start giving.
Here are some practical ways you can give to others.
Give them your prayers. Start giving by praying for the one who has offended you. "But I say to you who hear, love your enemies . . . **pray for** those who mistreat you." (Luke 6:27-28) He is not suggesting that we complain to God for the way we have been treated — pray for the person who offended you to grow and for you to see them *as God does*!

100

Prayer always breeds intimacy. If you pray for an enemy, they won't be your enemy for long — God will cause you to see something good in them and you will come to actually appreciate them!

Give them acts of kindness. These might include things as simple as a smile, a conversation, a card of appreciation, a visit, a gift, etc. If you will do the steps outlined here, they will prepare your attitude so that your giving is done with a heart of joy! Allow the Holy Spirit to direct you in this step.

Give them an opportunity to restore trust. When someone fails you, there is a temptation to write them off and never trust them again. That is not God's way. However, there is danger when you restore trust too quickly. Give people the opportunity to prove themselves again.

We are not commanded to trust people blindly. Trust is something that is earned, not freely given. "Let these first be tested; then let them serve." (1 Timothy 3:10) Our gift to all people is the **capacity** for trust. We should give all people the opportunity to prove themselves without being too suspicious.

Let's say that a husband gets involved in an adulterous situation. Should the wife ever trust him again? The answer is yes. But, unlike the other aspects of forgiveness, trusting someone who has violated a trust should be done with some reservation — in a trust-test-trust fashion — until the person proves himself again.

The principle of trust is: you meet a person, you trust them to a degree; and if they prove faithful, your trust grows. If someone has gone through this process, gaining your full trust and then later violates it, they must be made to go through the process again.

Unforgiveness just writes people off and does not allow them to go through the process again, once there has been offense. That is not right. Forgiveness, on the other hand, allows another chance. Still, forgiveness does not bypass and **should never** bypass the process of rebuilding trust. That would be foolishness.

Having to go through the process of building trust a second time after proving yourself once is humiliating. That is part of the process of repentance. If someone is unwilling and says, "Why don't you trust me? Haven't you forgiven me?", I would question if they were fully repentant or just sorry for getting caught.

This is especially true when dealing with ministers who have fallen. To get into the ministry there is quite a list of prerequisites found in the scriptures (Viz. Matthew 20:25-28; Acts 16:1-3; 20:28; II Corinthians 2:17; 4:1-2; 6:3; 1 Timothy 3:2-4; II Timothy 2:15; Titus 1:6-8; etc.). The Bible addresses everything from how they conduct their private lives to the reputation that they have with outsiders.

If a minister's personal life caves in, repentance and restoration is relatively simple for him or her as a person and as a Christian. But to reinstate him in ministry without some requalification would not be wise for the *man* or the *ministry*. Thank God that we serve a God of restoration and that failure does not mean we lose our usefulness in the Kingdom of God. Yet, we must *restore* ministry trust and that restoration is a **process** that takes some time.

Going back to our question of should the wife of an adulterer trust him again. The answer was *yes* —— with qualification.

How should she approach this? She shouldn't have to concern herself worrying about him and wondering if he is up to something. She should have the freedom to *question* him. If he comes home later than usual after work, she should ask him what happened. Keep in mind that a simple explanation should be accepted. Asking for an explanation is not to be an *interrogation*.

It is not wrong for the wife to want to know where her husband can be reached, and to expect him to call when he is late. She shouldn't let him cry, "You don't trust me." She did once, and he violated that trust. She *should* remain open to him **earning** that trust again because of forgiveness, but not without his proving himself.

When Jesus was dealing with people, the Bible says, "But Jesus, on His part, was not entrusting Himself to them, for He knew all men." (John 2:24) We don't have the luxury of "knowing all men," but we do have the Biblical precedent to "test" them (1 Timothy 3:10). **Trust must be earned!**

Forgiveness always releases a person from the act of offense, whether they are sorry or not. However, giving a "second chance," is predicated upon a repentant heart and should only be given as many times as the person is truly repentant.

Give Them Confrontation

"If a brother sins against you, **go to him privately** and confront him with his fault." (Matthew 18:15, TLB). When there has been conflict there usually must be some direct confrontation. Remember, when God dealt with Adam and Eve in the fall, He got to the root of the problem first — Satan. But then He dealt with **Adam and Eve**!

"And the Lord God said to the serpent, 'Because you have done this, cursed are you . . .' (Genesis 3:14)

"To the woman He said, . . . (V. 16)

"Then to Adam He said . . ." (V. 17)

When tension arises we must bind Satan, but it is equally important to deal with the people who have been involved in the conflict *if* they need to repent. Examples would be when a person commits action sins against you like stealing, actively sowing discord and lies, adultery, etc.

Many folks wrongly steer away from confrontation and it ends up being destructive in their relationships.

Bill Hybels writes, "Tenderhearted people will go to unbelievable lengths to avoid any kind of turmoil, unrest or upheaval in a relationship. If there's a little tension in the marriage and one partner asks the other, 'What's wrong?' the tender one will answer, 'Nothing.' What he or she is really saying is this: 'Something's wrong, but I don't want to make a scene.' In choosing peace keeping over truth telling, these people think they are being noble, but in reality they are making a bad choice. Whatever caused the tension will come back. The peace will get harder and harder to keep. A spirit of disappointment will start to flow through the peace keeper's veins, leading first to anger, then to bitterness and finally to hatred. Relationships can die while everything looks peaceful on the surface!

"Peace at any price is a form of deception from the pit of hell. When you know you need to tell the truth, the evil one whispers in your ear, 'Don't do it. He won't listen. She won't take it. It will make things worse. It's not worth it.' If you believe those lies, there is a high probability that you will kill your relationship sooner

104

or later."[4]

One of the best ways to love someone is to act in their best interests. That often means you must leave the comfort level of the relationship to deal with something that will be in the best interest of the other person. That is not easy to do. Confronting people is often very frightening.

When Not to Confront

Other times, when people do and say things inadvertently, they do not need to be confronted. Often, confronting a person is more of a temptation than wisdom. We are tempted to tell them how they hurt us or wounded us to somehow "get back" at them or make them feel badly.

Confrontation is not wisdom when we are not in the appropriate position to confront the person. A man confronting another man's wife on her attire; a parishioner approaching a visiting minister to correct his theology; unwanted correction of someone else's child, etc., are all inappropriate confrontations.

There are times, in an attempt to secure their own forgiveness, people feel they must confess their sins to the one they have sinned against. If it is an action sin, like those mentioned above, where you have violated a trust or need to give restitution, then do it. But if the other person has not really been affected, do not confront them.

I have been approached several times over the past twenty years as a leader in the Body of Christ by people who confessed they had a problem with me. The story usually goes something like this: "Brother Ed, please forgive me!"

"For what?", I ask.

"Well, I have had a real problem with you over the past six months and yesterday I finally got it resolved."

"What did I do?" I query, sort of bewildered, feeling my emotional guard arriving for sentry duty.

"Oh, never mind, I'm free now!"

The problem is —— now I'm not free! Then I race through my dealings with this person. "What have you done, Edwin?", I ask myself. At times I was tortured for days trying to figure out what I had done to offend them.

Confronting a person about your personal struggles with them is not wisdom and may, in fact, end up hindering their lives.

Let me go to Dr. Stanley again and relate the following from his book, *Forgiveness*; "Confessing our forgiveness to someone who has not first solicited our forgiveness usually causes more problems than it solves. I will never forget the young man in our church who asked one of the women on our staff to forgive him for lusting after her. She had no idea he had a problem with lust, and his confession caused her to be embarrassed and self-conscious around him from then on.

"I rarely counsel people to confess their forgiveness to those who have hurt them if the other persons have not asked for it. Once we begin to understand the nature of forgiveness, it becomes clear why this principle holds true. God forgave us long before we ever asked for it.

"We should confess our forgiveness if one of two situations occurs. First, we should confess our forgiveness if asked for it. This helps clear the other person's conscience and assures them that we do not hold anything against them.

106

"Second, we should confess our forgiveness if we feel the Lord would have us confront others about their sin. Their sin may have been directed against us personally or against someone we love. It may be necessary in the course of conversation to assure them that you have forgiven them and are coming more for their sake than your own. When we confront others about their sin, the issue of forgiveness must be settled in our own hearts. We must never confront in order to force another to ask for our forgiveness."[5]

When giving the gift of confrontation, make sure it isn't a bomb you are delivering! Wrap it with wisdom.

How to Confront
Before you actually sit down to confront a person make sure you deal with yourself first. Start by *clarifying the issue*. Is it really something that is important or are you just being touchy or picky? Is it something that will resolve itself after the person gains more experience or is it a permanent issue that pervades the way the person lives? If you feel you must deal with it, what do you feel is the real root of the problem?

Secondly, *surrender to God*. Galatians 6:1 says, "Brothers, if someone is caught in a sin, you who are spiritual should restore him gently. But watch yourself, or you also may be tempted." We must watch ourselves so that we do not succumb to the temptation to jump on others in a judging or criticizing fashion instead of employing *gentleness*, as this verse commands. If you feel angry or restless and you want to deal with the issue immediately, be watchful — you can end up hurting people as easily as helping them in this arena. Surrender your heart to God first. Tell Him you will sit tight until you sense His grace for wisdom, peace and kindness dawning within you.

Thirdly, *pray about the time and place* for the confrontation. It is important to find the appropriate time and place to share the "seeds" of confrontation. Ecclesiastes 3:2 says there is "a time to plant." Just as a farmer waits for the *right season* to plant as well as the best *place* for the seed —— we must be sensitive to time and place. During a television commercial or in front of the children are not good examples of time and place.

A farmer would never run out to the field to plant during a tornado or violent thunderstorm. Don't try to plant new ideas or perspectives that you feel are important during emotional tornados and thunderstorms. When your husband comes home for the day and his mind is still reeling from issues at work, don't try to confront him. While your wife is cooking or dealing with the children, the only input she is open to is you rolling your sleeves up and helping out —— don't try to confront her there. Late at night, when you are both tired is not a good time.

The conditions of time and place can make or break a confrontation situation. Set aside a special time to be together and go to a quiet place (i.e. favorite restaurant, go home early while kids at school, out for a walk, etc.). As an employer I often have to confront those who work for me. Time and place are paramount issues to me. I try to go to someone when they are not under excessive work or personal pressure and in a place where they feel the most comfortable. Seldom do I ask someone to "step into my office." Generally I will confront them in an "Oh, by the way . . ." fashion as we are walking from one side of our complex to the other, or I will step into *their* office and sit in front of *their* desk. The *time and place* secret is key to effective confrontation.

Dealing with yourself and selecting the right time and place for confronting a person is a big part of the battle. You win the rest of it when you approach the person with *honesty, care, and vulnerability.*

Start your conversation by *affirming your commitment to the relationship.* Everyone is listening for the "bottom-line." What is it that you want? Are you threatening them with an ultimatum? By affirming your commitment it helps them to see that you are interested in resolving **a problem,** not in getting your own way in a situation.

Tell your spouse how much you love and need him or her and that your marriage is the most important thing in the world to you. Tell your boss that you appreciate the opportunity to work with them or a fellow employee that you enjoy being on the same team. Tell a friend that you really appreciate their friendship.

Next, *carefully state the issue without placing blame on anyone.* Avoid broadbrush statements like, "you have always" or "you never." The moment you do that the other person's defense mechanisms start turning on and they no longer hear what you are saying. It is easy to brush off absolute statements like "you never." Even though a husband may have only helped his wife around the house ONCE in the first month of their marriage, he will write off her accusation that he "never" helps around the house as "extreme" or "blown all out of proportion." It is better to stick with statements like, "I feel alone. I feel that you are blocking me out —— that I don't matter. It's as if nothing I say has any bearing on where we are headed. It's confusing to me." The "I feel" phrases will get you a lot further than the blaming "you" phrases will.

Lastly, *encourage and invite dialogue.* After you have gotten the issue on the table, ask them, "What do you think? Am I all wet on this? Do you see any validity in what I am saying?" Honestly long for and value their perspective. Some folks will just write you off, others will go into shock that you have confronted them, still others will open up, immediately repent, and ask you to forgive them. No matter what the result is, it is always better to confront than it is to leave a relationship in a lie.

Forgiveness is a Supernatural Act

As you have read the preceding steps, you may have been tempted to say, "I can't do that!" The truth is . . . you are right! Forgiveness is a supernatural act that can only be facilitated by the power of God. That is why God's choice to *anoint* us with the Holy Spirit in our relationships is so significant!

Acts 1:8 says, "But you will **receive power** when the Holy Spirit comes on you." When Jesus was anointed by the Holy Spirit Luke 4:14 says, "Jesus returned to Galilee in the **power of the Spirit**." The anointing gives us the **power** we need to carry out the steps of forgiveness! *True* forgiveness is not possible apart from the hand of God in your life. You may be able to partially forgive, do one or two of the steps we've described, but total unconditional forgiveness is the result of God's enablement or anointing in your life, not of your own human volition.

9

FORGIVENESS: AN ACT OF VIOLENCE

Many in the Church fail to understand the real nature of forgiveness. Often it is viewed as a passive action taken by a person who is unwilling or unable to defend himself. But when you understand forgiveness, you realize that it is not a weak thing.

When you choose to forgive, you are not *overlooking* the actions of people so they can continue to offend you without being held accountable. Forgiveness is actually an aggressive force!

Forgiveness: A New Strategy for War

God has *wrath* in His nature. That wrath was never intended to be used against people, but against evil. However, if a person clings to the evil that God condemns, they get hurt. Listen to a description of God we don't often hear: "The Lord is a man of war: the Lord is his name." (Exodus 15:3, KJV)

God loves people but He hates evil. Before Jesus came, there was no way to separate people from evil, so when God came against evil, *people were destroyed.*

That is the reason for the flood. God did not hate those people; He hated evil and had to do something about it. Throughout the Old Testament, He commanded His people to do something about it as well.

"When the Lord your God shall bring you into the land where you are entering to possess it, and shall clear away many nations before you, the Hittites and the Girgashites and the Amorites and the Canaanites and the Perizzites and the Hivites and the Jebusites, seven nations greater and stronger than you. And when the Lord your God shall deliver them before you, and **you shall defeat them**, then **you shall utterly destroy them**. You shall **make no covenant** with them and **show no favor** to them." (Deuteronomy. 7:1-2)

The nations that lacked a covenant relationship with God could only be *cut off* or destroyed before Jesus' death at Calvary. God's people were commanded to rise and destroy the evil, which in that day meant destroying the people as well.

When a false prophet came into their midst, they dealt with him mercilessly. "But the prophet who shall speak a word

112

presumptuously in My name which I have not commanded him to speak, or which he shall speak in the name of other gods, **that prophet shall die**." (Deuteronomy 18:20)

Adultery was not just passively allowed. "If there is a man who commits adultery with another man's wife, one who commits adultery with his friend's wife, the adulterer, and the adulteress **shall surely be put to death**." (Leviticus 20:10)

If you offended your neighbor, you received retribution. "And if a man injures his neighbor, just as he has done, so it shall be done to him: fracture for fracture, eye for eye, tooth for tooth; just as he has injured a man, so it **shall be inflicted on him**." (Leviticus 24:19-20)

Disobedience and disrespect to parents were not tolerated. "And he who strikes his father or his mother **shall surely be put to death**. And he who curses his father or his mother **shall surely be put to death**." (Exodus 21:15,17)

The men and women of God in the Old Testament were a *warring* people. They were not to lie down and let wicked people or nations overrun them.

It is true we are living in a time when we do not have to violently come against *people* like they did in the Old Testament. The miracle of the cross opened the way for God to separate men from the evil they do. We no longer attack people, but does that mean we are to lay down and be overrun by evil?

I do not believe God wants us to think our warring days are over! We are still to be men and women of **war**. The only difference between those who battled in the Old Testament and those of us called to battle in the New Testament is *HOW* and with *WHOM* we battle.

113

Now we realize by the revelation of God that: "Our **struggle** is not against flesh and blood, but against the rulers, against the powers, against the world forces of this darkness, against the spiritual forces of wickedness in the heavenly places." (Ephesians 6:12)

We still have a struggle, a battle; but it is not against spouses, children, parents, friends, pastors, etc. It is against the forces of darkness that motivate people to do evil. Our warring is not against human beings, or flesh, but against Satan and his kingdom.

"For though we walk in the flesh, we do not **war** according to the flesh, for the **weapons of our warfare** are not of the flesh, but divinely powerful for the **destruction of fortresses**. We are **destroying** speculations and every lofty thing raised up against the knowledge of God, and **we are taking every thought captive** to the obedience of Christ." (2 Corinthians 10:3-5)

"Finally, be strong in the Lord, and in the strength of His might. Put on the **full armor** of God that you may be able to stand firm against the schemes of the devil."

Look at the warring terms used in these passages; *war, weapons of our warfare, destruction of fortresses, destroying, taking captive, armor.* We are still to be men and women of violence! We are still warriors of the King, called to go forth to secure His Kingdom in the earth, destroying darkness and "turning the world upside down" everywhere we go.

Forgiveness Opposes the Aftermath of Offense

Leo Buscaglia writes, "I recently heard of a woman in Florida who was raped, shot in the head, brutally mutilated and left to die. Astoundingly, she survived the ordeal. Her head wound left her permanently blinded. In a television interview the host was reflecting on the bitterness she must feel, the unhealing scars she would have to deal with for the remainder of her life. Her astonishing reply was something to the effect of, 'Oh, no! That man took one night of my life, I refuse to give him one additional second.'"[1]

I am not sure whether this woman really forgave the man or was just blocking him out, but the story illustrates the fact that incidents that violate us should not be allowed to linger in our minds after the event has taken place.

The forces of darkness, however, want us to focus on these negative events. Satan wants to capitalize on the offenses that come into our lives in the hope that he can propel us into envy, strife, confusion, anger, resentment, etc. By so doing, he can control our lives.

The Scripture says, "For where **envying** and **strife** is, there is **confusion** and **every evil work**." (James 3:16, KJV) I am convinced that Satan and the forces of darkness are just as interested in influencing us *after* an offense comes as they were in instigating the incident to begin with!

It is the potential aftermath of an offense that is the most destructive for us. If you and I could see into the spirit world, I believe we would see demons ready to pounce **after** an abusive event has come into a person's life.

It is here that we see the first aspect of the power of

115

forgiveness. **Forgiveness protects our lives from Satan's strategy by violently opposing the evil that tries to enter after an offense comes.**

Choosing to forgive (or release) an offense paralyzes the hand of the enemy because forgiveness "sends away" the incident. Just like God forgives by sending our offenses "as far as the east is from the west" (Psalm 103:12), we are to put the offense out of our thoughts. It is precisely this "sending away" of the incident that frustrates the enemy and prevents him from fouling up our lives any further!

Paul said, "If angry, beware of sinning: let not your irritation last until the sun goes down, and **do not leave room for the devil**." (Ephesians 4:26-27, Weymouth Translation) We "give place" to the devil when we *focus* so much on an offense that it effects how we feel and act.

It is being irritated by the incident "until the sun goes down" day after day that gives Satan place. It is **our focus** on the incident that leaves room for him.

Satan wants to dishearten and ultimately devastate us by keeping us focused on what happened. He loves to keep running "instant replays" of the event in our minds. His scheme is to get us to fester over our losses until our stomachs are eaten away by ulcers and we are obsessed with the idea of trying to "get even" with our offender.

To forgive, though, is to focus on **Jesus** instead of on the **offense**. Therefore, in forgiveness the incident loses its strength and the evil behind the episode is obliterated! This is the first violent aspect of forgiveness.

There is a verse that seems to apply here from 1 Corinthians 15:55, "O death, where is your victory? O death, where is your sting?" Forgiveness pulls the "sting" out of the incident that should have brought death. It is able to crush the disfiguring power of relational dysfunction. Forgiveness, like a protective bubble, keeps incidents of offense from becoming life-destroyers.

Paul explained how the actions of others did not have the power to destroy him. "We are afflicted in every way, but not crushed; perplexed, but not despairing; persecuted, but not forsaken; struck down, but not destroyed." (2 Corinthians 4:8-9)

What would be anyone's natural response to affliction? Most of us would be crushed emotionally. Yet why did the afflictions of Paul not crush him? When perplexity comes, don't we naturally despair? Not Paul. When persecution comes, don't we feel forsaken and alone? Yet Paul knew he wasn't forsaken. When struck down, the temptation is to quit and to allow our effectiveness to be destroyed. But not Paul. Why couldn't the people that brought affliction, perplexity, persecution and physical harm keep Paul down?

Because he realized his struggle wasn't against "flesh and blood." He knew he wasn't fighting people and he wasn't about to give Satan any foothold in his life by blaming them and letting his "irritation last until the sun goes down."

Paul effectively overcame the evil behind the offenses that came his way. He deflected Satan's ability to "sting" him through the actions of others. Paul knew forgiveness was a powerful weapon that would stop the forces that motivate men to do wrong.

God can send people like this to reach out to cruel people because they know how to destroy the evil behind what motivates a person's meanness. That is why God used men like Stephen. Stephen knew the power of forgiveness knowing both its devastating impact on the forces of darkness and its blessing to people.

Stephen prayed as he was being stoned, "'Lord Jesus, receive my spirit!' And falling on his knees, he cried out with a loud voice, 'Lord, do not hold this sin against them!' And having said this, he fell asleep." (Acts 7:59-60) How could he have done that? As much as I know about this subject, I would have been tempted to get angry with those religious bigots. Why didn't he get mad at them and call down judgment from heaven . . .

Because he realized he was not dealing with just the people he saw. He knew there were evil forces driving that crowd and refused to bow to the pressure of that evil. He knew that by separating that crowd from what they were doing, and loving the people while hating the sin, he would devastate the evil forces behind them and bring God's enablement for repentance to the people.

The evil forces behind the crowd could not cause Stephen to get angry, resentful, or bitter. The evil that motivated them was powerless to make him react wrongly. The power of forgiveness kept him free from the "sting" of this inhuman act.

When Jesus called us to a new kind of living in Matthew 5, He was not asking us to be doormats for the human race! Jesus was beginning to show us how to live in a fallen world without being emotionally destroyed. "Do not resist him who is evil; but whoever slaps you on your right cheek, turn to him the other also. And if anyone wants to sue you, and take your shirt, let him have your coat also," and so on.

He was showing us that through forgiveness we are protected from the evil actions of men. We can turn our cheeks because we are not offended and crushed by the enemy's blows.

We can give our coat and our shirt to those who sue us because we know where our source is and we know that if others take all our things they will only leave us in the arms of a loving Provider. We obey Matthew chapter 5, not because we are to be passive pawns in the hands of offenders, but because we have the violent strength of forgiveness.

It may look like we are going down when we give up our rights to obey Matthew 5, but in the end we come out a winner. It looked like Satan won when he crucified the Lord, but he didn't know the plan for the following Sunday morning.

We don't have to fear and to defend our rights when we are being attacked. We can forgive our offenders because we know something they don't . . . Sunday's comin'!

Be watchful here! You may be tempted to feel superior to a person that you have forgiven, just because you were generous enough and wise enough to do so. That is not true forgiveness.

True forgiveness does not try to make a point, put you on top or make you look good. True forgiveness is done in obedience to God in response to what He has done for us. David Augsburger wrote, "When 'forgiveness' puts you one-up, on top, in a superior place, as the benefactor, the generous one, the giver of freedom and dignity —— don't trust it, don't give it, don't accept it. It's not forgiveness; it's sweet saintly revenge."[2]

When we forgive, we are winners over the forces of darkness and their schemes, *not over people*. Remember our *struggle* is not with them anyway! The believer should never think in terms of winning and losing when dealing with another person!

Notice Jesus' words again: "Do not resist **him** who is evil." The issue of this verse is that we do not have to fight **with the people** that are *vessels* of evil —— we are bigger than that. But we *are* to attack the **evil** itself aggressively and violently.

Remember, the people who offend us do so for various reasons: their fallen nature, the devil, the influence of a secular world filled with evil, misunderstanding, etc. The violence of forgiveness does not make the people who have offended us look bad, or pay back the wrong they have done. The violence of forgiveness deals with the **evil** behind why people do what they do.

Forgiveness Fosters Change

The second violent aspect of forgiveness is that it releases the power of God toward offenders so that God can change them.

Oswald Chambers wrote, "If I receive forgiveness and continue to be bad, I prove that God is immoral in forgiving me, and make a travesty of Redemption. When I accept Jesus Christ's way He transfigures me from within."[3]

The same holds true in our forgiving of others. If we forgive only to be nice, we are making ourselves nothing but doormats to be trampled upon again and again. That is not what forgiveness is intended to do!

When we forgive, God's holiness and rightness flows through our actions and attitudes toward the offender! Paul addresses this in his letter to the Romans. He writes,

"Never **pay back** evil for evil to anyone. Respect what is right in the sight of all men. If possible, so far as it depends on you, be at peace with all men. Never take your own **revenge**, beloved, but leave room for the **wrath** of God, for

120

it is written, '**Vengeance** is Mine; I will **repay**, says the Lord.' But if your enemy is hungry, feed him, and if he is thirsty, give him drink; for in so doing you will **heap burning coals** upon his head. Do not be overcome by evil, but **overcome** evil with good." (Rom. 12:17-21)

Paul uses violent terms. *Pay back. Revenge. Wrath. Repay. Heap burning coals. Overcome.* The forgiveness we described in chapter six is not a mealy-mouthed, spineless, wimpy thing to do because we don't have enough guts or sense to stand up for ourselves!

Forgiving someone is "turning the other cheek" or looking to God to avenge the wrong done to us instead of taking matters into our own hands with natural retaliation. Somehow this enables God to move within that person to overcome the evil that is dominating their lives.

A story from the life of Smith Wigglesworth captures this truth. Wigglesworth was a world-famous evangelist who ministered during the late 1800's and early 1900's. The story is about how Polly Wigglesworth, Smith's wife, dealt with him when he was allowing his heart to grow cold.

"In those days of much business and prosperity, his attendance at religious services declined, and his heart began to grow cold toward God; but the colder he became, the hotter his wife became for God. Her evangelistic zeal never abated, nor her prayer life. Her quiet, consistent Christian life and witness made his laxity all the more apparent, and it irritated him. One night a climax came.

"She was a little later than usual in getting home from the service and when she entered the house, he remarked: 'I am the master of this house, and I am not going to have you coming home at so late an hour as this!' Polly quietly replied, 'I know that you are my husband, but Christ is my Master.' This annoyed him and he put her out the back door. But there was one thing he had forgotten to do — to lock the front door. She went around the house and came in at the front door laughing. She laughed so much that he had to laugh with her; and so that episode was finished.

"When some husbands backslide, their wives get sour and nag at them from morning till night, but that was not the way of Polly Wigglesworth. She had a merry heart, and while she was on fire for the Lord, she made every mealtime a season of fun and humor. And she wooed her husband back to the Lord and to his oldtime love and zeal for God."[4]

Why wasn't Polly Wigglesworth offended by her husband's behavior? No doubt they had been to other meetings together where they were just as late getting home. Why didn't she defend herself? Why didn't she begin to huff and argue saying, "You wouldn't care if you weren't so backslidden!"? Why didn't she run to her folk's place after being thrown out of her *own house?* Why didn't she file for divorce because her husband was "hindering her ministry?"

Because forgiveness protected her!

Forgiveness is a powerful thing. We must realize that the evil that men do is not just done on their own — there are evil forces behind their hurtful actions. Then we must choose to love the person in spite of their actions. This releases a power that no evil force can endure! The result of Polly Wigglesworth's forgiveness was the destruction of the evil that was motivating her husband to backslide! Once that force was halted, he immediately returned to his original commitment to Christ.

Everyone would serve Christ with a whole heart if the forces of darkness would be kept in check! "If our gospel is veiled, it is veiled to those who are perishing, in whose case the god of this world [Satan] has blinded their minds." (2 Corinthians 4:3-4)

Forgiveness is a miracle of God's grace —— a powerful thing. It has dominion over evil and darkness. Through forgiveness God reigns over the past in our lives. A forgiven man does not have to continue having his future painted with his past.

But God's forgiveness toward us does not stop there. For me, the greatest miracle of His forgiveness is how God enters through forgiveness to destroy the potential for evil in us and then gives us strength to face the future as changed individuals.

I know forgiveness has a violence in it because I am a forgiven man. Every time God has forgiven me, I have touched His holiness and something transforms me in that moment. The evil that drove me to sin is no longer there —— it is obliterated! Chambers wrote in another book, "Forgiveness is a miracle, because in forgiving a man God imparts to him the power to be exactly the opposite of what he has been: God transmutes the sinner who sinned into the saint who does not sin."[5]

Yes, temptation will reappear and failure may result, but each time we return to Him, the fresh power of forgiveness restores and refires us for victorious living.

Think this through for a moment. Paul said, "For the work of the cross is to those who are perishing foolishness, but to us who are being saved **it is the power of God**." What happened at the cross? The cross is the cornerstone of forgiveness. Notice that the "power of God" was released at the same place forgiveness was birthed! Forgiveness is not a weak thing. Through forgiveness, He blasts out the wrong in our lives and reigns with His goodness in our lives!

When we forgive people the way God forgives us, we release the power of God to destroy the evil that motivates them to do wrong.   This is spiritual warfare at its best.   Armed with forgiveness, we must see ourselves in a position of authority with God's power. As His representatives we must rise up and get involved with the lives of people.

We are the "light of the world!" Light always destroys darkness. We are not to "participate in the unfruitful deeds of darkness, but instead even expose them" (Ephesians 5:11). God never wanted His children to be compromising, non-confrontational beings that wander the earth just-a-hopin' for the rapture to come.

We are to be His love warriors, blasting away the evil that dominates the people of this age!   Jesus said, "These signs will accompany those who have believed: in My name they will **cast out demons** . . ."! (Mark 16:17)

In the December 1988 edition of Voice, the magazine of the Full Gospel Business Men's Fellowship International, there is a story of how one man gained victory through the power of forgiveness. Charlie Osburn not only experienced the protection of forgiveness, preventing him from being destroyed over an offense, but he also experienced the power inherent in forgiveness to transform his offender. The story follows.

"'Daddy, I want to show you the fun we've been having,' my eight-year-old daughter smiled as she dropped the magazine in my lap. 'We've done some of the things they show in here.'

"Within a few seconds, my skin crawled. My little girl had handed me the filthiest pornography I had ever seen. It was so perverted you couldn't even buy it at the newsstands where they routinely stocked that kind of trash.

"My next-door neighbor was a child molester. As the ugly story unfolded, I discovered that not only had he raped and molested my daughter for two years, he had victimized my son.

"Since my wife had been busy running our popular restaurant, our two youngest children stayed with him and his wife after school. We had every reason to trust him. We had known him for years and his children had grown up with my wife.

"For eight long years after the crimes, I hated that man. But soon I learned that hatred is the deadliest poison you can allow into your system. If you don't flush it out, it will destroy you.

"I had him arrested and tried, but since he was 65 years old, the jury recommended sympathy. The judge gave him a 10-year suspended sentence, placed him on probation and sent him home.

"'God, how I hate him!' I seethed the day the last board went up on the eight-foot-high fence I erected to block my view of his house.

"Part of the reason for my intense reaction when I learned my kids had been assaulted was the belief that the incident would ruin my treasured civic career. This prompted me to spend more time at home; but my children quickly grew to resent my new overbearing and suspicious attitude.

"My unresolved hatred also fanned such flames of animosity that I began drinking heavily in a vain attempt to soothe the rage. I wanted to kill my neighbor, and fantasized about bombing his car, hiring a hit man, or tossing a torch on his house late at night. Fear of the death penalty was the only thing that stopped me.

"However, this raging kettle of emotions didn't help my marriage either. As the gulf between us widened, I decided to leave. I had a girlfriend in the real estate business, so I figured I could join her and let my wife have the restaurant.

"Then something happened that I hadn't bargained for - I failed the real estate exam. While I was back in town studying to take it again, I ran into Father James Smith, a priest I had met when I joined the Catholic church. Assigned to another parish, he had been away for 14 years.

"'Well, praise the Lord, Charles,' he grinned when I greeted him at our restaurant. When he asked how I was, I spent two hours moaning about my problems. Afterwards he replied, 'Charlie, I've got good news for you.'

"He told me Jesus loved me totally, completely and unconditionally, in spite of myself. For a month I wound up going to the rectory to see Father Smith every week. We talked for hours at a time.

"'Charlie, you've got to give it all to Jesus!' he shouted every time I walked into his office. Finally I yelled back, 'Tell me what to give Him and I will!'

"He prayed with me that day to receive the baptism in the Holy Spirit, but after more counseling and prayer, he showed me Matthew 6:14-15 and Luke 6:27-35, the passages where Jesus talks about forgiving and loving our enemies.

"'You mean I have to love the man who molested my children?' I asked. 'Why, he's a horrible human being! Even the thought of loving him makes me ill.'

"Finally the priest asked me which was worse, rape or murder. I answered, 'Murder, of course.' With that he flipped to 1 John 3:15, which equates hatred with murder.

"I brooded over his words for three weeks. Then, I saw my neighbor by accident. We lived on a one-way street and he drove by as I was backing out of my driveway. I hesitated, then yanked the key out of the ignition and ran after him. When I approached him in his driveway, he threw up his arms in front of his face and pleaded, 'Don't hit me!'

"'I'm not going to hit you,' I said. Then, I forced the words out. 'I've come to ask your forgiveness for hating you.'

"Hallelujah! No sooner had I said it than I felt lightheaded. My inner emptiness had vanished. The pain that throbbed in my chest was gone, too. Physical healing was budding forth in my body. How good it felt!

"Leaving my neighbor with a slightly stunned look on his face, I ran home and asked my children for their forgiveness, since my over-reaction and the resulting family tension had caused as much damage to them as the molestation.

"That healed my relationship with my youngest daughter, but it took awhile for my son to reach reconciliation. When he finally accepted Jesus six years later, he said, 'Thanks, Dad, for loving me into the kingdom!'

"With this festering spirit of hatred and unforgiveness abolished, I was ready to receive the Baptism that Father Smith had talked about. It happened a few weeks later as I was driving down the highway. Suddenly I knew — I knew that I knew that I knew that I knew — that Jesus was the Lord of my life.

"I pulled off the road, lay down on the seat and raised my hands towards heaven. When my own vocabulary was exhausted, I began to pray in a wonderful, strange tongue, praising God in His own language and worshiping Him in Spirit.

"Forgiving the man I'd wanted to kill: that simple act of

obedience unlocked a door to a personal relationship with God that is so wonderful, so powerful, so joyful that I've been shouting ever since!

"Then another dramatic incident occurred. Three months after I forgave the man and asked him to forgive me, my wife saw him in the supermarket. He beamed as he showed her his New Testament, telling Jeanne how he had given his life to Jesus. Three weeks later, he died."[6]

Friend, forgiveness is a violent act against the evil that dominates people. Because of its power over evil, it protects you from being destroyed by the offenses of people as well as promoting change in the nature of the offender. Hallelujah!

You may scream, "I could never forgive a person like that!" You are right. Neither could Charlie Osburn. When Charlie felt imprisoned by unforgiveness, God did a work inside him that enabled him to release his transgressor. Charlie had to make the choice to obey God and forgive the man, but God undergirded and enabled the decision, making it a reality. Forgiveness is not a human thing; it comes from God.

Corrie ten Boom spent a large part of her life as a prisoner in the concentration camps of Nazi Germany during the Second World War. She saw unspeakable acts committed against innocent human beings —— including those done to her own flesh and blood sister, who was eventually murdered. She writes this,

"In the concentration camp where I was imprisoned many years ago, sometimes bitterness and hatred tried to enter my heart when people were so cruel to my sister and me. Then I learned this prayer. It's a thank-you based upon Romans 5:5.

"Thank You Lord Jesus that You have brought into my heart the love of God through the Holy Spirit Who was given to me. Thank You Father that Your love in me is victorious over the bitterness in me and the cruelty around me.

"After I prayed it, I experienced the miracle that there was no room for bitterness in my heart anymore. Will you learn to pray that prayer too? If you are a child of God, you have a great task in your prison. You are a representative of the Lord Jesus, the King of Kings. He will use you to win others for Christ.

"You can't, you say? I can't either. But Jesus can! The Bible says, 'Be filled with the Spirit.' If you give room in your life to the Holy Spirit, then He can work through you making you the salt of the earth and a shining light in your prison."[7]

Faith is the inborn capacity
to see God behind everything.
Oswald Chambers

10

GROWING THROUGH OFFENSE

What if the person refuses to change? When do we stop forgiving?

God's decision to forgive us is unconditional. In other words, it is not dependent on whether or not we respond. The Holy Spirit comes to convince us of sin and of the forgiveness available through Jesus Christ (John 16), but God never violates a person's will.

Many who have been confronted with the conviction of the Holy Spirit respond by hardening their hearts instead of opening them. There is an old saying that goes, "The same sun that softens wax, hardens clay." One thing is certain, there is always change when God moves upon people — *they* determine the nature of that change.

We too must forgive people unconditionally. We must recognize that the person is not the problem, separate them from their sin, make a decision to release them from the debt they owe us, and begin to give to them. We must do this with an expectation that "burning coals" are being "heaped upon their heads" or that the fire of God to cleanse and change them is at hand.

But we must also be aware that they may refuse God's hand and continue to be the way they have been, or even grow worse. It has been my personal experience that people get hardened before they break and soften up. People may be slow in changing and you may need to forgive repeatedly as offenses continue to come your way. Remember that in the process of forgiveness the offense loses its ability to affect you adversely. So, even if the perpetrator chooses to harden his heart to God's cleansing "fire," their evil is neutralized as far as you are concerned.

The Benefits of Forgiving Others

There are so many beneficial things that you can learn from being a forgiving person — even if others refuse to change. For one thing, you learn to throw yourself more on God in living trust because you are not demanding all your needs to be met by others through their right actions.

You develop a better understanding of the price Jesus paid to reach out to you as you reach out to others in His Name. You begin to understand His patience toward others as you choose to patiently forgive and stay with them.

Because of the good that will come when we trust God in the

midst of offense, you can actually come to the place where you laugh when relational adversity comes your way! (Remember Polly Wigglesworth?)

When you maintain a forgiving lifestyle, you begin to think like Joseph did in the book of Genesis. His brothers had done him wrong. He was sold into slavery by them and grew up apart from his family in a foreign land. Instead of growing bitter and choking off the blessings of God in his life, he chose to forgive and to continue obeying God. Because of his obedience, God exalted him to a high position in Egypt.

By the time he met his brothers again, the very ones who had robbed him of a normal life, he was in a position to get revenge. But Joseph did not try to "get even" with them as they bowed before him trembling. He said, "Do not be afraid, for am I in God's place? And as for you, you meant evil against me, but God meant it for good in order to bring about this present result, to preserve many people alive. So therefore, do not be afraid; I will provide for you and your little ones." (Genesis 50:19-21)

What an incredible perspective! This is fulfilling the command to "not be overcome with evil but overcome evil with good" (Romans 12:21). Forgiveness gives us the perspective that every time a person does something to us "for evil," God is able to turn it around and "mean it for good."

Forgiveness enables us to see that with God's hand, an evil act can result in helping "preserve many people alive" instead of destroying them like Satan intended. Whether the offender ever changes, forgiveness still wins because it neutralizes the result of evil in our lives and opens the door for the resurrection of good!

A person who matures in the arena of forgiveness is a great asset in the Kingdom of God. God can send him or her on "covert" missions to get close to people who are very difficult to deal with. If you are unable to be around people because you are easily offended, you will receive assignments that only weak people can handle.

I have always been baffled with Christians who only want to work with other Christians. Why would you want to do that? If God calls you there, fine; otherwise, get out there among the unregenerate slobs! That is where the action is!

We have to settle it. As long as we live in a fallen world, we will have the opportunity to be offended. How we deal with it is the issue at hand. Either we deal with offense spiritually and become "love warriors" for God, or we deal with it naturally and get trapped into things like envy and strife which lead us to a life dominated by Satan — a life filled with "every evil work." (James 3:16)

If you are going to have successful relationships you must know how to deal with offense once it comes. But restoring relationships is not an end within itself. The relationships that bring joy don't "just happen," they have to be *cultivated* and *developed*.

God uses men who are weak and
feeble enough to lean on Him.
Hudson Taylor

11

ANOINTED RELATIONSHIPS

When God first spoke to me about my relationships being *anointed*, it seemed pretty strange to me. I thought that the anointing was reserved for spiritual areas, so, I never expected to be anointed in my relationships.

The term *anointed* implies an "upon" presence of the Holy Spirit. "Upon" suggests the idea of pressure from above. When you are *anointed* you are being pressed upon by the Holy Spirit to think and act differently than you would have alone. This anointing not only affects you as the "anointed one," it also releases power to change those you are ministering to while under the anointing.

If you are like most of us in the charismatic/pentecostal world, you would think the anointing applied to things like preaching in a pulpit, winning thousands to Christ on the mission field, being on a church staff, raising the dead, healing the sick, studying the Bible, operating in the gifts of the Spirit, etc. . . . the general spiritual things we know about and see the preachers do.

But on that day in the spring of '82 I described to you in Chapter One, I couldn't deny it. The anointing was there. God's power was present and it was having an effect on my attitude, thoughts, and actions. During that visitation I wondered why God would be interested in anointing me to be sensitive and gentle to my wife? Then He spoke to me. He said, "You are operating in the office of a husband."

I knew what an office in the kingdom of God was. I stood in one as a minister. As I preach, pray, and oversee services, I am constantly looking to God for His enablement or help. I don't look to my intellect or ability, but for the "upon" presence of the Holy Spirit.

The person who stands in the *office* of President of the United States is not influential because of who HE is. He is influential because of the strength the office holds. In the same way, a man or woman who stands in the office of an apostle, prophet, evangelist, pastor or teacher is not influential because of *who they are* but because **there is an anointing** for those offices. That anointing gives them the influence and the results. Isaiah said, "The yoke shall be destroyed **because of the anointing**." Isaiah 10:27. In other words, it is the anointing that gets results, not man's ingenuity.

To stand successfully in the *office* of a pastor, for example, you must face the position looking to Jesus for enablement and direction. An infant is unable to feed, clothe or care for itself —

the baby must look to its parent. In the same way, the one who stands in an office of ministry must see his or her utter helplessness apart from their heavenly Parent.

I had learned to face ministry that way, but when God said I was operating in the *office of a husband*, it sort of threw me. This wasn't the ministry . . . this was my "Ordinary Zone." Aren't I responsible to be a good husband and dad!? I don't need God here like I do when I preach or minister to the sick, do I!?

The "office of a husband." That just did not make sense. I said to the Lord, "Where is that in the scriptures?" He said, "Go to Ephesians 5 — you'll see it there."

And there it was. In verse 18 Paul says, "And do not get drunk with wine, for that is dissipation, but be filled with the Spirit."

Literally translated, the latter part of the verse reads, "and **be ye being filled** with the Spirit." I knew being filled with the Spirit of God constituted an "office" of God because it meant you were full of Him and representing Him not yourself.

The next verses tell us **how** we are to be "being filled" with the Spirit.

The Office of a Priest

Verses 18-20 talk about being filled with the Spirit as we worship and sing to the Lord from our hearts with thanksgiving. I had experienced that. I knew how to bring God's presence into my life through worship and praise. As I read this the Lord spoke, "That is the *office of a priest*."

Remember I Peter 2:9? "But you are a chosen race, a **royal priesthood** . . ." Hebrews 13:15 tells us what we are to offer as sacrifice. "Through Him then, let us continually offer up a

sacrifice of praise to God, that is, the fruit of lips that give thanks to His name."

This means that we can be being filled with the Holy Spirit and sense His anointing whenever and wherever we worship! As you vacuum your carpet, stand in the office of a priest and enjoy being lifted and filled with the wonderful presence of the Holy Spirit. As you work in the factory, sing under your breath with all your heart. You'll feel His anointing and refreshing as you do.

You don't have to be an apostle to have the hand of God on your life. You don't even have to wait to go out witnessing to sense His love. The same God who said, "You shall receive power when the Holy Spirit has come upon you; and you shall **be My witnesses** . . ." is also the one who said, "Be being filled with the Spirit . . . **by singing and making music in our hearts to the Lord**." This is the *office of a priest.*

The Office of a Servant

In verse 21, God shows us another way to be "being filled" with the Holy Spirit, constituting another office; "And be subject to one another in the fear of Christ."

I am certain that every Christian has experienced the joy and flow of the Holy Spirit that comes from selflessly serving other people. This is the *office of a servant.*

Thank God that in the past decade we have seen the ministry of helps brought to the forefront. No longer do men and women approach the various ministries in the church (i.e., greeting at the door, ushering, leading people into praise and worship, etc.) by looking to their own talents and abilities. We have learned that God values those areas and that there is an enablement or anointing that flows from heaven for people who participate in them.

Folks have discovered you don't have to preach in a pulpit or be a missionary evangelist to sense God using you in a meaningful way in Christian ministry!

But the offices that exist for God to anoint us for effective ministry and service don't stop at the doors of the church —— He is interested in equipping and enabling you in the ordinary areas of your home and place of employment!

The Office of the Wife and the Husband

In verse 22 of Ephesians 5, God continues to show us ways we are to "be being filled with the Holy Spirit": "Wives, be subject to your own husbands, as to the Lord . . ."

As a woman takes on the perspective that is put forth in these verses, she can literally release a flow of God into her marriage that is not unlike the flow of God to teach from a pulpit, the flow of God to heal when hands are laid on the sick, or the flow of God that inspires as we witness to the lost. The same Spirit flows, but the results are different.

Here in the home, the *office of the wife* is for building (See Proverbs 14:1). A woman anointed by the Spirit can build her husband and children and make the home the closest thing to heaven on earth! Referring to the home in Deuteronomy 11:21, God said that our days would be ". . . as the days of heaven upon the earth."

God values the home! He calls heaven a *home* and Himself a *Father.* The truth is that the home existed **before** the church, before the Fall. When God made man, He did not create them to start a church. Adam and Eve were not the first pastors. They were a husband and wife, and they had a home. The church was not instituted until *after* the Fall and it was God's answer to the Fall.

If He anoints preachers to preach in the church, why wouldn't he anoint those who stand in positions of responsibility and authority in the home? Since the church is only as good as the homes that are involved, I believe the home is a high priority with God. There **is** a supernatural anointing available for our homes.

Verse 25 shows how the man can "be being filled with the Spirit" in the home. "Husbands, love your wives, just as Christ also loves the church and gave Himself up for her."

As with the wife, if a man takes on the perspective that is put forth in these verses, he can literally release a flow of God into his marriage that is not unlike the flow of God that is experienced in other offices and operations of God. The same Spirit flows but the results are different.

The *office of a husband* is one that leads and provides in the home. The husband should take the initiative when forgiveness, discipline, kindness, attention, or communication is needed. He is not just a provider with finances. Men, enabled by the Holy Spirit, are to meet the needs of their families spiritually, mentally, emotionally, physically, socially and financially.

Ephesians 6:1-3 shows us that even a child can participate in "being filled with the Spirit" *as they obey their parents.*

Ephesians 6:4 introduces us to the *office of a parent.* As I learned about these various anointings, I purposed to operate in them. I have had days filled with His presence as I have been with my children. His anointing has caused me to be more consistent

140

with my children, in terms of discipline and training.

I have actually been filled with gladness as I have done foolish things with them, like playing ball, bike riding, or fishing — things that I used to think were a waste of energy and poor stewardship of time. I have sensed this anointing as I sat looking at my children, trying to capture the memory of how they looked at this age. Once as I was doing that, God spoke to me about how much He enjoyed watching *me* and participating in *my* life — He was discipling me while I was enjoying my children!

Another time He spoke to me and said, "If you will approach this time with your children under my anointing, you will grow in Me as much as you would have if you spent an equal amount of time studying My Word." I didn't really believe it at first, but it worked. He spoke volumes into my heart as I wrestled and played with my toddlers on the floor. It was great!

The Offices of Employee and Employer

The *office of an employee* is seen in Chapter 6 starting in verse 5, "Slaves [employees], be obedient to those who are your masters [employers] according to the flesh, with fear and trembling, in the sincerity of your heart, as to Christ."

The office of the employee is for demonstrating the Christian's love for God in how he or she works. There is a flow of God that is released in the work place as the employee does his or her work as though God directly asked them to do it, and they do it "filled with the Spirit" with all their heart.

And finally, the *office of the employer*. "And masters [employers] do the same things to them [the same way the Christian employee should do what he or she does unto the Lord,

141

so should the Christian employer], and give up threatening, knowing that both their Master and yours is in heaven, and there is no partiality with Him."

In each of these offices, the person is to look helplessly to heaven, but the offices are different in scope and in the way they operate.

As I have learned to walk in the anointing in these everyday arenas, it has enriched my life in many ways. Three ways, however, stick out the most to me.

First, living under these anointings related in Ephesians chapters 5 and 6 have helped me **to value what God values**. He only anoints areas that are important to Him. I have learned to place a higher value on my wife and children, and on the people with whom I work.

I no longer take them for granted or try to "use" them as pawns for my "visions." I *invite* them to participate in what God has called me to and have great respect and awe for their personal uniqueness and contributions. I am also more committed to *helping them* fulfill their God-given destinies.

Secondly, this anointing **has brought some SUPER into my natural**, making it more SUPERnatural. My ordinary life that was filled with predictable, boring duties and obligations suddenly became an adventure! Life has become a joy instead of just a daily grind. I'm not saying that I do not continue to have rough spots, I am saying that with these anointings I press through with a note of victory and joy within. It seems that the little things in life have become a thrilling expedition instead of a "have-to" and a burden.

In 1 Peter 3 starting in verse eight, the Apostle Peter begins to sum up the Christian life. By this point in the text, he has discussed the great trials these believers were experiencing and the conflicts they were facing on the job and in the home — the ordinary places of our lives. He concludes the following:

(V. 8) "Finally, all of you, live in harmony with one another; be sympathetic, love as brothers, be compassionate and humble.

(V. 9) "Do not repay evil with evil or insult with insult, but with blessing, because to this you were called so that you may inherit a blessing.

(V. 10) "For, "Whoever would love life and see good days must keep his tongue from evil and his lips from deceitful speech."

Notice from verse 9 that God called us so that we may "inherit a blessing." I believe a great part of this "blessing" is God's anointing upon the believer to press through the trials and conflicts of life and relationships without being defeated.

The result is found in verse 10. Because of the "blessing" of God, we don't have to respond to life with an "evil" tongue or with "deceitful speech," but we can really "love life and see good days." Do you realize how many people hate their lives? Do you realize how many people have bad day after bad day? No joy. No peace. Many are like zombies "just going through the motions." Their lives seem like retakes of the movie, *Night of the Living Dead.* There are Spirit-filled people who live like this!

Richard Exley writes, "What about those Christians who are

faithful, who have godly families, who are successful in business, yet know little or nothing of real contentment, not to mention the Abundant Life. Those, who in their heart of hearts, live with a secret disappointment. They wouldn't admit it to anyone, maybe not even to themselves, but life hasn't been all they expected. Marriage, children, career success, and even Christianity have all failed to produce the promised return. What about them?

"Jesus said that He came to bring us abundant life (John 10:10), yet most of the Christians I know are living on the ragged edge. Oh, they have their moments, but, for the most part, it's hard to distinguish the quality of their lives from that of the unregenerate."[1]

When speaking of the curses that would come upon the nation of Israel for their disobedience to God's law, the Scripture says,

"There the LORD will give you an anxious mind, eyes weary with longing, and a despairing heart.

"You will live in constant suspense, filled with dread both night and day, never sure of your life.

"In the morning you will say, 'If only it were evening!' and in the evening, 'If only it were morning!' —— because of the terror that will fill your hearts and the sights that your eyes will see." (Deuteronomy 28:65-67)

The curse of the broken law involved a sense of desperation and discontent! In the morning, they wished it were night. In the evening, they wished it were morning. In modern vernacular, the grass was always greener **on the other side**!

"If only I were married to a person like . . .". "If I only had a job like . . ., then everything would be OK." If I only lived over in . . .." If only my parents hadn't . . ., I would be able to . . .." This "I'd rather be" thing is a curse!

According to Galatians 3:13, "Christ redeemed us from the curse of the law." We don't have to have any of the curses that fall upon those who live in disobedience!

Psalm 23 says, "The LORD is my Shepherd, I shall not be in want. He makes me **lie down** in green pastures." It didn't say, "He makes me climb fences, change locations, and meet new people, to find **green** pastures!" The world may say, "The grass is greener on the other side," but our God says we can **lie down** in the green pastures. In other words, when we let Him shepherd our lives, He makes *where we are* the best place to be!

Even though your marriage, family, church, business, finances, and personal well-being may be on the driest, deadest looking grass in the world, Jesus will help you! You don't have to get a new marriage, new family, different church, new business, etc., because things seem dead and better elsewhere. Let God shepherd you!

I think the miracle of contentment is one of the greatest miracles we can present to get the attention of a dying world in need of Christ.

Thirdly, this anointing brings God's kingdom on the scene to effect a change in how things are. The kingdom of God is not an idea or an intangible force like "Mother Nature." The kingdom of God is the place where dramatic things take place — a place where God settles in and **His will is done**!

Jesus said in Matthew 12:28, "But if I drive out demons **by the Spirit of God**, then the kingdom of God has come upon you."

Whenever *anything* is done "by the Spirit of God" the kingdom of God comes! The kingdom is His influence and reign.

I am tired of seeing Satan and *his* kingdom reigning in the marriages, homes, churches, and personal lives of believers. It is time for us to discover and begin walking in the anointings of God that will evidence God's kingdom and His will in our lives!

You need not cry very loud;
    He is nearer to us than we think.
                                   Brother Lawrence

12

THE ABC'S OF THE ANOINTING

I don't want to just know *how* to live right; I want to live right. But the commands of God for making relationships work and our lives complete are beyond a "decision" or human "will power." Christianity is impossible to live —— apart from Christ.

Jesus said in John 15:5, "Apart from me you can do nothing." But with Him Philippians 4:13 says, "I can do everything through Christ who gives me strength." And how does Christ give us strength? By the Holy Spirit. Now we are back full circle to the anointings listed in Ephesians chapters 5 and 6.

If you have been used by God in ministry or have been a worshipper you will understand when I say that it takes some time to learn *how* to tap into the anointing of God for any area.

Here are three secrets I have learned that have enabled me to deliberately move into His anointing. I call them the ABC's of flowing in God's anointing and they work for any area that God promises to anoint from preaching to facing Monday morning at work.

"A"ccept

If you are going to flow under the anointing of a wife, or husband, or as a pastor, or worshipper, you must **accept** that the anointing is available for **you**.

Galatians 3:2 says, "I would like to learn just one thing from you: Did you receive the Spirit by observing the law, or by **believing what you heard**?" The first key to receiving the anointing of the Holy Spirit is to believe that it is really there and that God is longing to give it to YOU!

It is obvious that He wants us to have it because He commands us in Ephesians 5:18, "Be filled with the Spirit." Why would He command you to have something He wasn't longing to give you?

This **acceptance** is not a passive thing, where you wait around to see if God will show up. I had a visitation where that happened, but that is not God's best any more than Saul of Tarsus falling on the ground with a great light in Acts 9 is the general way for people to get saved!

This **acceptance** needs to be a contending and aggressive acceptance. You refuse to take anything less than God's best. The Scripture says in 1 John 2:20 and 27, "But you have an anointing from the Holy One . . . As for you, the anointing you received from Him remains in you . . . But as His anointing teaches you about all things and as that anointing is real, not counterfeit —— just as it has taught you, remain in Him."

Husbands, when you have had a bad day and you want to go in the house and be a selfish slob, sit in your driveway and contend for the anointing of a husband. Thank the Lord that no matter how you feel you believe that there is an enablement from heaven, an anointing to help you walk into your home with victory and joy. Decide to walk into your home "under the influence" of God instead of under the burden of the day. Decide to bring the kingdom of God and His will into your home and it will become a glorious place instead of a habitation of hell.

Ladies, when you are not getting your needs met because of the insensitivity of your husband and you feel like he is the dweeb of the universe, stop and contend for the anointing of a wife. Thank God that no matter how you feel you can tap into His enabling power to walk into your marriage to build instead of tearing it down with wrong actions, attitudes and words. Trust God to flow through your kindness and prayerful confrontation so that godly change can come into your home.

Parents, when you are tempted to choke your children for the communist plot they have designed to destroy your life, contend for God's anointing for parents. The parenting anointing enables you to be patient and kind, yet firm. When you get to your breaking point, ask God to help you diffuse the situation and give you the wisdom to effectively deal with it.

There is an abundance of opportunities as employees and employers to contend for the anointings available in those arenas. Don't let His grace toward you be in vain (See 2 Corinthians 6:1). Let's contend to walk in these anointings so that Jesus is glorified!

149

"B"ow

If you are going to walk in these anointings you must realize that they are not humanly possible. They are from God. To tap into them you must look to God in absolute helplessness realizing that the best we can do on our own is mess up.

For years I was defeated as a Christian. I thought that Christianity was a result of intense commitments made by men and women better than me. Oh, I could be consistent for a while, but it was always such an effort that I would finally cave in. Then, it was back to the altar to try to make a stronger commitment than before.

Then I saw it. Paul said in Romans 7 starting in verse 21, "So I find this law at work: When I want to do good, evil is right there with me. For in my inner being I delight in God's law; but I see another law at work in the members of my body, waging war against the law of my mind and making me a prisoner of the law of sin at work within my members. What a wretched man I am! Who will rescue me from this body of death?"

The Apostle Paul was simply saying that Christianity is impossible to live. No matter how much you know, no matter how much you try; you will end up short. Christianity is not Buddhism or Hinduism. We can't just "decide" to live a Christian life!

Christianity is the supernatural result of a life open to the living Christ filling the human heart. Hence, Paul answers his own question, "Who will rescue me from this body of death?" with "Thanks be to God —— **through Jesus Christ our Lord!**"

To operate in the anointings listed in Ephesians we must **bow** and look helplessly to God for His enablement.

150

"C"onfront

Every time I have **accepted** the reality and availability of His anointing, coupled with a deep **bowing** within — knowing my utter helplessness — I was positioned to flow in the anointing. But, I have never sensed the anointing until I began to rise and **confront** the situation with Biblically defined actions.

As a husband, I **accept** His anointing and **bow** before Him, but I never experience the anointing until I *start acting* the way the Bible commands a husband to act.

A husband is to approach his home like Christ does the church. He is to view his wife like Christ views the church. Jesus is the "author and finisher of our faith." He is the one who is sensitive to our needs and watches over us. Even when we fail, 1 John 2:1 says that He is the one who initiates reconciliation and love. Christ's role to the church outlines the husband's role in the home. The husband is to be sensitive to the needs of his wife and children. He is to see himself as the initiator of forgiveness, love, and kindness.

The anointing for a husband is released when you begin to practice these perspectives and actions. You will not be perfect, to be sure, but regard the action steps you do take as cries to your Father for His enablement. No matter how inconsistent or incompetent you are here, your feeble attempts to fulfill the biblical commands as unto the Lord will result in the miraculous! James 2:26 says, "As the body without the spirit is dead, so faith **without deeds** is dead."

In my experience, I always had to **confront** my marriage, parenting, ministry, etc., *doing the best I could do* before God moved in with His anointing to undergird me and make the situation a joy. God flashes through our action steps in these things just like He flashes through us when we place our hands on the sick. Our hands really don't do anything but He still has chosen to flow through them. Our actions are weak at best, but He still has chosen to flow through them.

If you want to experience these anointings, you must **accept** that they are there and available for you. You must **bow** before Him, realizing you cannot do this on your own. And then you must do the best you can do to **confront** the situation with Biblically defined actions for that given area.

I know the plans I have for you, declares the
     Lord, plans to prosper and not to harm you, plans
to give you hope and a future.

Je 29:11 NIV

13

A PROPHETIC WORD

It wasn't until the early 1900's that the church experienced the dynamics of pentecost on a world-wide scope. The whole idea of anointed preaching is fairly new to the Body of Christ. For years men ministered out of their own intellect from the pulpit.

It is only in the past few years that we have seen the importance of the ministry of helps (the office of the servant) and of worship (the office of the priest) emphasized.

We have done what we have known to do, but we must press on so the church can be what Christ wants us to be as Ephesians 4:15-16 shows.

"We are to grow up in all aspects into Him who is the Head

even Christ, from whom the **whole body**, being fitted and held together by that which every joint supplies, according to the **proper working** of **each individual part**, causes the growth of the body for the building up of itself in love."

How can there be a "proper working of each individual" if they do not even know the offices that are available in which to "super" their natural? For them to "extra" their ordinary?

Ephesians 4, verse 1, urges us to "walk in a manner worthy of the calling with which you have been called." This epistle was not written to just professional ministers; it was written to the laity, the ordinary folk. There is a **calling** for ordinary people to walk in a supernatural way in their everyday lives!

You don't have to go to Africa to sense the hand of God using you and filling you . . . again, the same God who said, "Go ye into all the world" said, "Husbands love your wives." There are supernatural offices that God is calling believers to stand in. The equipping ministries in the body of Christ must place value on them in order for people to walk in them.

The call to those of us in full-time ministry in these last days is to honor what God honors, value what God values. There are some verses in 1 Corinthians 12 that seems to come across in a prophetic way to me:

"The eye [those in leadership] cannot say to the hand [followers], 'I have no need of you'; or again the head [leadership] to the feet [followers], 'I have no need of you.'"

"On the contrary, it is much truer that the members of the body which seem to be weaker [followers] are necessary; and

154

those members of the body, which we deem less honorable [followers], on these we bestow more abundant honor [we honor their places of service as priests, servants, spouses, parents, employees, or employers], and our unseemly members come to have more abundant seemliness,"

"Whereas our seemly members [those in full-time public ministry] have no need of it. But God has so composed the body, giving more abundant honor to that member which lacked, that there should be no division in the body, but that the members should have the same care for one another."

We should never think in terms of one being more important than the other. Yet, often those of us in full-time ministry have allowed ourselves to be made into heroes. We must not allow that! We are to place no greater value on the equipping office of an apostle than we do on the office of the wife (though the equipping offices, of which the apostle is a part, will impact many more people than the office of a wife is designed to do). Though they serve in completely different ways and produce different results, they are both valued by God!

The message of 1 Corinthians 12 is that we must purposely place greater honor on the offices that don't seem to have a dramatic effect and may even appear ordinary, mundane, and unimportant. This would particularly involve the offices that only affect the home.

As we place proper honor on things, the Body will not long for areas of service they are not called to just because those offices appear to carry a status that is enviable.

It is my belief that there are some in full-time ministry today, not because of the call of God, but because of a longing to be where God could really use them. Stepping into an area where they are not called stifles their fruitfulness. Consequently, the churches they serve are hindered — worse yet, the precious people who have stepped into ministry with sincerity and a longing to serve become disillusioned.

We have not honored the God-given offices of priest, servant, spouse, parent, employee and employer, so many have felt that the only effective place of ministry was as a pastor or another kind of full-time minister.

I'm convinced that every member in the Body of Christ would celebrate their lives if they knew how much God valued the ordinary and if they understood the anointings that were available to them to SUPER their natural. Such a celebration would surely rattle the gates of hell and draw millions into the kingdom of God!

*I find that doing the will of God leaves
me no time for disputing about His plans.*
                                    Macdonald

A FINAL WORD

Let me charge you one last time. Quit thinking, "If only my husband would . . .," "If only my child would . . .," "If only that person would . . .". Forget what everyone else is doing and rise up and start doing what you have just read — **even when you are not the one responsible for the mess to begin with!**

I spoke with a man from Florida who had drifted away from any kind of relationship with his two brothers. Actually, the brothers were at fault. They had ignored some of the casual ways this man had been reaching out to them, so he just quit trying. But the Lord wouldn't leave him alone, so he began getting more aggressive in reaching out to them. He told me, "I knew I was not wrong. I had done everything I knew to do to improve the situation. I eventually concluded that there was nothing more I could do — they had already rejected what little effort I had given. But in sheer obedience to God I began reaching out to them and quit looking for a response from them. I made an incredible discovery. When they saw my persistence, and after they became convinced that I was **committed** to reaching out to them **no matter what they did**, they began opening up to me. Now we have a great relationship!"

A friend of mine has a dad who is about as selfish as a person can be. He ran off with a strange woman when my friend was a young boy — so, father and son never had much of a relationship. About 13 years ago, my friend felt God wanted him to start building a relationship with his dad. At first it was a hard row to hoe because his dad doesn't know how to treat people (he has been through four marriages). It has taken time, but just recently his dad looked across the table at him while they were having lunch and for the *first time* in over thirty years told him with absolute sincerity, "I love you, son." Those words went into my friend like cool water into a sun-parched traveler.

Decide that no matter what condition your relationships are in you will keep fighting for their success. Too many of us give up without a fight when our relationships begin to disintegrate. Why is it that we will scrap and claw and even go to court to guard our possessions and yet roll over and play dead when relationships die? We are thinking wrong. Relationships are worth fighting for.

Conflicts might persist, sparks may fly, but in the end, with God's grace, you will "overcome evil with good." If you have ever seen or experienced the joy of restoring a relationship that was on "death row," you will agree with me that they are worth fighting for until you win!

Notes

Chapter Four
1. *Pulpit Helps*, June, 1988 issue; Chattanooga TN.

2. Exley, Richard, *The Rhythm of Life*; Honor Books, Tulsa, OK.

Chapter Eight
1. Stanley, Charles, *Forgiveness*; Oliver-Nelson Books, THomas Nelson, Inc., Nashville, TN; 1987.

2. Kittle, Gerhard, *Theological Dictionary of the New Testament*; WM. B Eerdmans Publishing Company, Grand Rapids, Michigan; 1983; Volume 1, pg. 509.

3. Godbold, Cash, *Scriptural Solutions for Sensitive People*; Sarasota, Florida.

4. Hybels, Bill, *Who You are When No One's Looking*, Intervarsity Press, Downers Grove, IL.

5. Stanley, Charles, *Forgiveness*; Oliver-Nelson Books, Thomas Nelson, Inc., Nashville, TN.

Chapter Nine
1. Buscaglia, Leo, F., *Loving Each Other, The Challenge of Human Relationships*; Ballantine Books, Randome House, Inc., New York, NY.

2. Augsburger, David, *Caring Enough to Forgive*, Regal Books, Ventura, CA.

3. Chambers, Oswald, *The Shadow of Agony*, Christian Literature Crusade, Ft. Washington, PN.

4. Frodsham, Stanley, H., *Smith Wigglesworth, Apostle of Faith*; Gospel Publishing House, Springfield, MO.

5. Chambers, Oswald, God's Workmanship, Christian Literature Crusade, Ft. Washington, PN.

6. Osburn, Charlie, *Voice*, Full Gospel Businessmen's Fellowship International, December 1988.

7. Boom, Corrie ten, *God's Plans are Perfect*, Quest Tape, Mobile, AL.

Chapter Eleven
1. Exley, Richard, *The Rhythm of Life*; Honor Books, Tulsa, OK.

For information about Ed Gungor's books, seminars, speaking
engagements, cassette tapes, and videos write:

Ed Gungor Ministries
P.O. Box 278
Marshfield, Wisconsin 54440

Additional copies of
Supernatural Relationships
are available from your local bookstore or by writing:

Harrison
House

HARRISON HOUSE
P.O. Box 35035
Tulsa, Oklahoma 74153

About the Author

ED GUNGOR is the senior pastor of Believers Church in Marshfield, Wisconsin, an itinerant instructor for Christian Life College of Theology, author, and sought-after speaker. He is known for his down-to-earth teaching style, presenting God's Word in a fresh, relevant way. For over 20 years, he has demonstrated a wholehearted commitment to helping Christians live their lives in a way that glorifies God. Ed has authored several life-changing books including *Turning Point* and *Peas in a Pod: The Miracle of Getting Along*.